HO RAILROAD
from start to finish

MODEL RAILROAD HANDBOOK NO. 36

BY JIM KELLY

SENIOR EDITOR

KALMBACH  BOOKS

The material in this book first appeared as articles in MODEL RAILROADER magazine. They are reprinted here in their entirety.

Contributors: Art Curren, Bob Hayden, Jim Kelly, Bill Morrissey, Gordon Odegard, Sam Swanson, Keith Thompson, Jeff Wilson

Published by Kalmbach Publishing Co., 21027 Crossroads Circle, P.O. Box 1612, Waukesha, WI 53187

HO railroad from start to finish / (compiled by Jim Kelly.
    p.   cm. – (Model railroad handbook ; no. 36)
    Includes index.
    ISBN 0-89024-155-4 : $11.95
    1. Railroads–Models. I. Kelly, Jim, 1940- . II. Title: HO
railroad from start to finish. III. Series.
    TF197.H57 1992   92-45817
    625.19–dc20   CIP

Contents

What started out as a piece of foam core grew gradually into an exciting and challenging layout anyone can build.

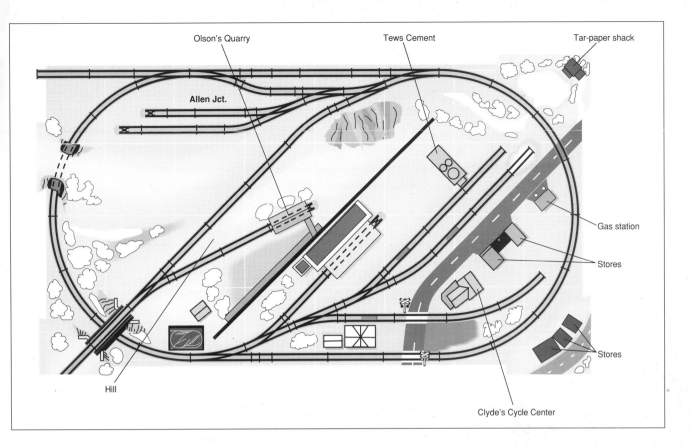

Olson's Quarry   Tews Cement   Tar-paper shack

Allen Jct.

Gas station

Stores

Stores

Hill

Clyde's Cycle Center

Introduction

In 1952 the staff of Model Railroader Magazine built a small HO railroad, the Pine Tree Central. Then they presented a carefully crafted article in the magazine showing the reader how he could build one for himself. This was the first in what became a long tradition of such efforts. We call them project railroads, and we're very proud that thousands of model railroaders have built them. Most have been small railroads, like the Cripple Creek Central featured in this book.

Traditionally a project railroad is carefully planned and built before a word about it appears in print. With this series, though, we decided to take a more spontaneous approach, to just jump in and start paddling. Each month we'd add something new, and we'd try to make it a project that any modeler might find interesting, even if he weren't building the Cripple Creek. We called the series "Especially for beginners." It became fun for both us and the readers to watch the layout grow from a loop of track on a table to a fairly sophisticated and attractive railroad.

I wrote most of the articles but other staff members also contributed — their names are on the chapters they wrote. I'm proud to say that two of the chapters were provided by readers who built models for the layout and mailed them in.

Because of our unstructured approach,

a final track plan didn't appear until the series was half over. Also, a complete list of the track we used never did appear. For your convenience, both are presented on these two pages. Also, many of you will want to use Atlas track. You'll find a track plan and list of track needed on pages 74-75.

Readers often ask how well the foam-core table we built for the layout has held up. I can only answer that after two years it's still going strong, has traveled to several shows, and shows no signs of warping. If you'd rather build a more conventional table, though, pick up a copy of Kalmbach's book *How to build Model Railroad Benchwork*. Be aware, though, that the Kato no. 3102 track set we used

includes 24"-radius curves, meaning a loop won't quite fit on a 4-foot wide plywood sheet. If you want to use Kato Unitrack on a 4x8 table, buy the track pieces individually, and use the no. 2210 21 5/8" radius curves instead. Once you've built a table you can take the remaining articles in just about any order you'd like. If you can't find a kit we used, substitute something else you like — do it your way.

On behalf of all those who worked on the "Especially for beginners" series I'd like to dedicate this book to our fond memories of the late Gordon Odegard. Gordy was a wonderful and enthusiastic colleague, but even more, he was a friend we could all count on.

Jim Kelly

Kato Unitrack used

1	3-101 HO standard track set
15	2-150* 9" straight track sections
5	2-120* 4 1/2" straight track sections
4	2-220* 24" radius curves sections
3	2-850 lefthand no. 4 turnouts
6	2-851 righthand no. 4 turnouts
4	5-101 track bumpers

* Kato sells track sections in boxes of 10. Call around and you may locate a hobby shop that sells these pieces individually.

The Cripple Creek Central includes all the elements of a first-rate layout but little of the complexity.

Building a foam core board layout

Our basic material is easily cut with a utility knife

BY JIM KELLY

Welcome TO our new series, "Especially for beginners." For the next year or so we'll be taking you step by step through the construction of a beginner's layout. Watch with us as the layout you see here grows.

In hopes of exploring new ideas and techniques we've laid some ground rules:
- Simple construction techniques
- No messy materials
- No power tools
- Lightweight materials that permit easy transport
- All materials transportable in a small car.

In short, this is a layout for the apartment dweller, someone for whom noise and mess are verboten, and someone who has little experience with using tools and building things. We'll keep an eye on expenses, but the criteria listed above count more than costs.

As in cat-skinning, there are lots of ways to build layouts. If you're brand new to model railroading, let me recommend one of our Kalmbach books, *Fun with Electric Trains,* for a quick and basic introduction. If you already have a grasp of the basics and want to proceed a bit further, then try *All Aboard: The Practical Guide to HO Model Railroading,* also from Kalmbach.

Okay, so right now it looks a little bare. Over the next year we'll finish this HO layout in a new series, "Especially for beginners." So look out world, this railroad is going to grow!

OUR FOAM CORE TRAIN BOARD

Beginner layouts are usually built on 4 x 8-foot plywood sheets, but that material couldn't meet several of the requirements listed above. Instead, we chose foam core, a material often used for making signs and displays. You'll find it at art supply stores.

Foam core is a super-light sandwich, a slice of expanded styrene foam served up between two layers of heavy paper. We used ½"-thick material purchased in three 40" x 60" sheets (small enough to get in a car, remember?). At nearly $20 a sheet the material wasn't cheap.

There's a big price break on ¼"-thick foam core, so you could save money and achieve the same results by using that and laminating the sheets together with yellow glue or contact cement.

Figure 1 shows how we cut up the foam core sheets. The rather unusual dimensions of the finished layout were dictated by the Kato track set we were planning to use — the loop it forms is a bit too wide to fit on the popular 4 x 8.

We cut the foam core with a utility knife. If you do the same, use three or four light passes per cut. It's easy to wander off line if you take a more

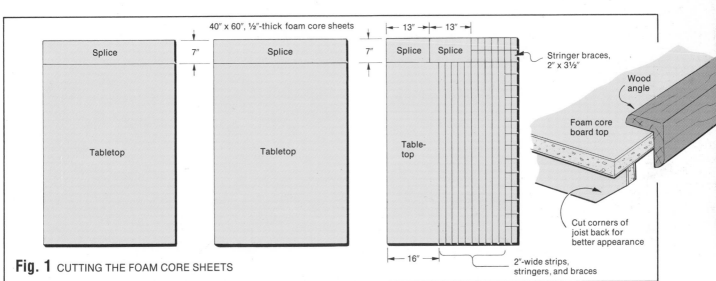

Fig. 1 CUTTING THE FOAM CORE SHEETS

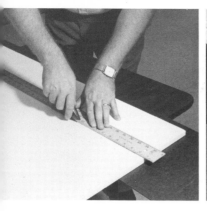

FIG. 2. ASSEMBLING THE TABLETOP

Left: We used a steel rule and utility knife to cut the foam core board, protecting our folding table's top with a scrap of Masonite.

Middle: We used Elmer's yellow carpenter's glue to cement the splice plates to the three top pieces. **Right:** Heavy books (in this case, bound volumes of MR) were used to weight the glue joints.

FIG. 3. ADDING JOISTS AND STRINGERS

Above left: We cemented our foam core joists in position, again weighting them with bound volumes. Spacing was arrived at scientifically — they're as far apart as bound volumes are tall! **Above:** Next came the stringers, using wood for strength. **Left:** Foam core blocks next to the stringers lock them in place. **Lower left:** Our author realized too late that the joist corners should be trimmed for better appearance. The Band-Aid on the left palm testifies to the wisdom of using a wood block to back the cut.

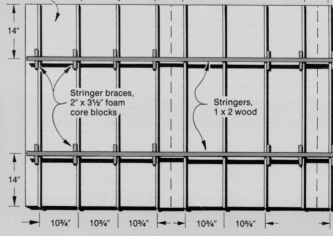

FRAMING PATTERN
Tabletop (see fig. 1)
2"-wide foam core joists
Splice plates
Splice plates
14"
Stringer braces, 2" x 3½" foam core blocks
Stringers, 1 x 2 wood
14"
10¾"   10¾"   10¾"   10¾"   10¾"   8¾"

FIG. 4. PAINTING
Left: Tan latex paint was applied with a roller. **Right:** Our table legs are cardboard boxes, painted flat black. Later the visible portions of foam core were also painted black for better appearance.

macho approach. Also, when you buy that knife, make sure to get extra blades — they do wear out. And you'll need a screwdriver for taking the knife apart for blade changes.

We joined the tabletop pieces together as shown in fig. 2, using yellow glue. (Yellow glue is better than white in this situation because white causes paper to swell.)

Next we added the joists and stringers, as shown in fig. 3, again using yellow glue and weighting the parts down until the glue set. For appearance's sake I went back and trimmed the corners on the ends of my joists. You'll be able to do a neater job by trimming them before installation.

The 1 x 2 wood stringers are the strongest part of the layout top, and you should use them as handles whenever moving the board. The foam core braces help anchor the stringers to the joists and add a lot of strength. Just don't carry this layout outside on a breezy day. It weighs only 18 pounds, and you've got a lot of sail area!

We roller-painted the board with flat tan latex paint, as shown in fig. 4. Pick a shade — on the light side — that you like. Don't throw the leftover paint out — later we'll use it to paint the ground when we add some scenery features.

The edges of the layout are wood angle, painted or stained to your liking. Ours is a stain called "pecan," followed by a semigloss polyurethane varnish.

Cutting the 45-degree corner angles on the wood trim is the toughest part of this project. One possibility is to have a picture-framing shop cut them for you. The distance between inside corners on the long sides should be 7'-10⅜"; on the short sides, 4'-3". I cut my corners with a miter box and backsaw, but working carefully you could accomplish the task with a modeler's razor saw, a tool you'll also find useful for later projects. Cement the angle on with your yellow glue.

We wanted an easy way to get the tabletop off the floor and considered several possibilities. Bookcases are good for this, as are sawhorses, but we settled on cardboard moving boxes, bought at a local U-Haul. These are the dish-type boxes and stand 27" tall. I put them together with U-Haul's box tape, then painted them flat black. I made four boxes, but two turned out to be enough, if a tad wobbly. Use four if you prefer.

USING UNITRACK

At last we're ready for the part of model railroading most of us like best, the "railroady" part, starting with the track. For this project we're using Kato's Unitrack starter set. All we have to do is join the sections together, and we instantly have the look of finished track. The ballast (those rocks that hold the ties in place) are cast in and don't have to be added later, as is the case with the sectional track most modelers use. (There's no free lunch, though — the Unitrack is considerably more expensive than sectional track.)

The hardest part of using the Unitrack set is finding the short curve section. Clue: look at the regular curve sections very carefully. Also, use a nail or other pointed object to push on the pins from underneath when you want to remove the little side fillers on switches and fitter sections.

ABOUT POWER PACKS

Many of you will be starting with a train set, and the power packs in these are usually not satisfactory. Control at the low-speed end is frequently poor, and often these packs deliver just enough power to handle the train that came in the set on the set's track loop.

Your hobby dealer offers good quality replacement power packs by MRC, Bachmann, and other manufacturers. Generally these run between $25 and $50, depending on the features. You want one with a large, easy-to-control knob or handle that will deliver excellent train control at very low speeds.

Oh, and don't throw that set pack away. Chances are it'll come in handy someday for powering an accessory.

For now our track is just laying on our layout loose — we may want to make some changes, but we did cut holes through the foam core to drop the hookup wires through it. As fig. 5 shows, this is easily done with our hobby knife. Anytime we want to move track and a hole is exposed, we can just cement a small piece cut from an index card over it and paint it with our tan latex paint. A very nice feature of the Unitrack system is that all the wiring can be dropped straight down under the track and totally hidden.

FIG. 5. WIRING
Left: To drop the hookup wires through the table, we pushed the track aside and cut a hole. **Right:** Here's the power pack shoved aside to show the holes for the power cord and hookup wires.

Products used

Adhesives, paints, and stains
Flat black latex paint, 1 quart
Flat tan latex paint, 1 quart
Semigloss polyurethane varnish, ½ pint
Wood stain, ½ pint
Yellow carpenter's glue, 1 pint

Foam core
½" x 40" x 60" sheets, 3

Hardware
Small wire nuts, 1 pkg.
22-gauge zip cord, 1 roll

Wood
1 x 2, 8 feet long, 2
1⁵⁄₁₆" angle, 8 feet long, 4

Tools

Awl (or large nail) for poking holes in foam core
Hobby knife and no. 11 blades
Hobby razor saw
Paint pan and roller
Screwdriver
Utility knife and blades
1" throwaway paint brushes, 2
3'-0" steel rule

Train supplies (HO scale)

Atlas locomotive (S-2 or other)
Kato Unitrack track set
Mantua "Heavyweight" cars, 3

POWER AND TRAINS

Our power pack is a Spectrum Magnum from Bachmann. It's a modern transistorized controller and delivers .90 amps. Most modern HO locomotives require only about .25 amps, so we have enough power to run three or four engines — more than we'd ever want to run on such a small layout anyway.

Again, we were able to install the power pack neatly in the corner of the layout by cutting holes down through the foam core.

The turnout included in our track set can be controlled remotely or by a tiny hand throw down on one side. The turnout controller was made to plug into the side of a Kato power pack, but not knowing that and having already bought our Bachmann pack, we'll cement it in position next to the controller. Our yellow glue will hold it, although admittedly not well.

Figure 6 shows how we handled the one little wiring challenge we had. The wires from the turnout weren't long enough to reach the control, so we cut them with the hobby knife and spliced in a length of 22-gauge zip cord purchased at Radio Shack. We can complete our wiring splices with small wire nuts (usually color-coded black). This method is just fine for a small layout like this, and we'll use it throughout the project.

And now, friends, we can run a train. Our engine is an Atlas S-2 switcher, an excellent product and completely ready to run. The same goes for our cars, "Heavyweights" by Mantua. You'll easily find less expensive ready-to-run cars, but you won't find any as good. In model railroading, just as in anything else, you get what you pay for. Steer clear of bargain equipment, and let your hobby dealer help you make good choices.

Trains, tracks, power, and a table to put them on — the basic elements of model railroading. Next month we'll add some structures and a hint of scenery. ✿

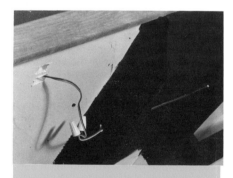

FIG. 6. EXTENDING WIRES
Plastic wire nuts were used to splice extensions into our turnout control wires, eliminating the need to solder. It's easy to poke holes through the foam core joists with an awl and run wires neatly through the layout

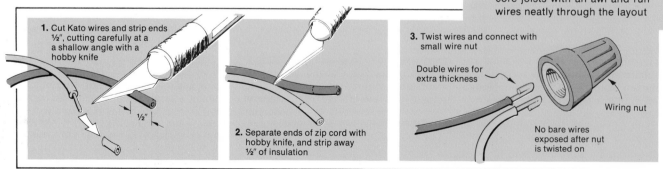

1. Cut Kato wires and strip ends ½", cutting carefully at a shallow angle with a hobby knife

½"

2. Separate ends of zip cord with hobby knife, and strip away ½" of insulation

3. Twist wires and connect with small wire nut

Double wires for extra thickness

Wiring nut

No bare wires exposed after nut is twisted on

Building plastic structure kits

Weathering-as-you-go techniques for added realism

BY JIM KELLY

WHAT'S LEFT to do on the HO scale railroad we started last month? Well, darn near everything! This month we'll get away from the stark naked look by adding two buildings and sowing some grass seed.

It just seems natural to start with a station because that's the place where people and trains most often get together. Our first kit, then, will be Atlas' no. 706 station. This building is a model railroading classic that's been around at least 25 years. It was designed by Steve Schaffen, founder of Atlas, and Ted Stepek. The station's lines absolutely smack of railroading in the eastern and midwestern United States anytime from the turn of the century on.

GETTING ON WITH IT

This is a medium-difficulty plastic kit with something a bit out of the unusual — excellent instructions! Just read them through once, then follow them, and all should go well.

A few words of general advice:

● For a neater job, resist the temptation to twist the parts off the sprues. Cut them free with a hobby knife, wire cutters, or even fingernail clippers. See fig. 1.

● After removing the parts from the sprues, it's a good idea to clean them up with a large flat file.

● Check that the parts fit properly, with no gaps, before cementing them together. Sometimes a burr or a bit of flash will prevent a good fit. Get after the perpetrator with your knife or file.

● Use a liquid cement for plastics, and apply it sparingly with an artist's brush, as shown in fig. 2. Capillary action will draw the cement into the seam. This cement is really a solvent that softens the surfaces being bonded so they will stick together. Too much liquid cement can only distort the parts or mar the surfaces.

Although the Testor's cement we list in the products used will get the job done, it's good to have a second, faster-setting brand for situations where you want the bond to set up extremely fast. Tenax-7R fits the bill here.

Our finished station is shown in fig. 3.

We built the station and cement plant for our HO layout from medium-difficulty plastic kits. Chris Becker photo.

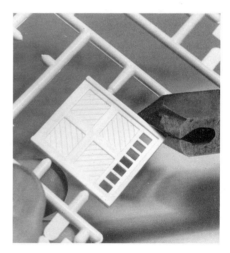

FIG. 1. FREEING PLASTIC PARTS
Above: Side-cutters work very well for removing plastic parts from the casting sprues. A hobby knife or a razor saw is also good.
Below: Flat files, available at hardware stores, make short work of smoothing edges.

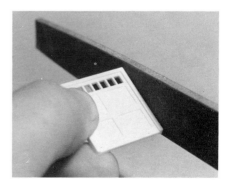

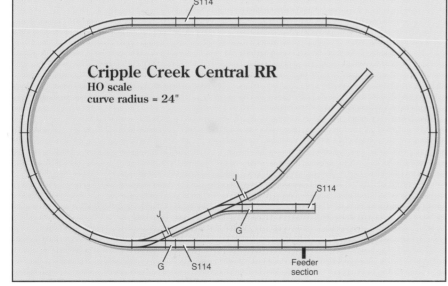

Cripple Creek Central RR
HO scale
curve radius = 24"

S114

S114

J

J

G

G

S114

Feeder section

All in all it went pretty well. The telephone booth was hard to get together. If you find it getting on your nerves, just throw it away! Who needs the aggravation? Also, the roof braces didn't fit as well as we'd like. About all you can do here is trim and file on the tabs that slip into the wall until they finally go. Just take your time.

We didn't paint the station, but we did decide to paint the roof after the building was finished. That big shiny expanse of gray shingles quickly became much more realistic-looking, so this little job was well worth the effort.

To paint yours the same, first apply brown sparingly, dipping the brush in the paint, wiping some off on a paper towel, and brushing down the roof. The idea is to let some of the dark gray show through.

After the brown has dried, drybrush the shingles with Khaki. To do this first wipe practically all the paint off the brush on a paper towel, then brush down lightly so as to highlight the grain and edges.

THE READY-MIX CEMENT PLANT

The station gives our railroad the beginnings of a headquarters — a place

Fig. 3. Quick now, which half of the roof looks better? If you say the left, you're breaking our hearts. We've drybrushed the right side with Polly S paints to improve its appearance.

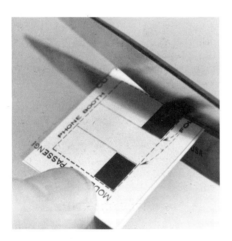

FIG. 2. GLAZING WINDOWS

Above: We tend to forget about them, but common ordinary scissors are the best tool for cutting acetate and other thin sheet materials. **Below:** Liquid plastic cement is best applied with an artist's brush. Capillary action draws the cement into the seam.

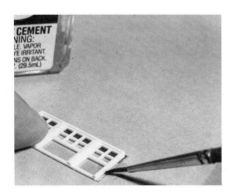

Products used

Atlas
706 station kit

Faller
B-950 cement mix plant

Kato Unitrack
EP550-R, right-hand turnout, 1
S246 straight track sections, 3
R610 curve section, 1

Life-Like
1071 Scene Master light green ground cover

Polly S paint
410013 Grimy Black
410030 Reefer Orange
410070 Roof Brown
410082 Concrete
500011 White
500060 Khaki
500074 Brown
501997 Stainless Steel

Woodland Scenics
T63 coarse turf, light green

X-acto
No. 1 hobby knife
790-11, five no. 11 blades

Miscellaneous
flat file, 8" long
small paint roller
Tenax-7R plastic cement
Testor's liquid cement for plastics

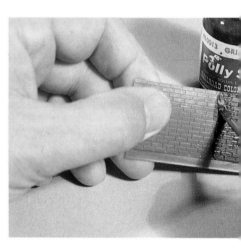

FIG. 4. ADDING MORTAR

Above: We painted the walls with black Polly S acrylic paint. Other colors could be used. **Below:** When the paint was about half-dry (ten minutes later), we wiped off the block surfaces with bits of paper toweling, leaving black mortar in the joints.

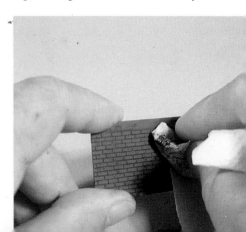

Fig. 5. Here's our completed cement plant. All the subassemblies, the green tanks, for example, or the platforms, were given color washes and allowed to dry before final assembly.

to work out of. Now we need some place for cars to go.

Just because we saw it in the hobby shop and it looked neat, we'll build the Faller Ready-Mix plant. This time we'll incorporate some "weathering-as-you-go" techniques to make the structure look more realistic. We have no quarrel with the kit's colors, just those shiny surfaces.

Figure 4 shows how we added some mortar to the block walls in the kit. The natural temptation is to make mortar white, but look around you in the real world and you'll see that the real stuff is tinted every color imaginable.

We detailed the brick walls further by painting a few individual bricks here and there with different colors, using Roof Brown, Khaki, and Orange. You need paint only a few bricks with these off-colors to perk up the walls.

To kill the shine on the plastic parts we used an old trick borrowed from master builder Art Curren, scrubbing the parts with a mildly abrasive household cleanser, such as Comet or Ajax.

After scrubbing the parts, we washed on a little color while they were still wet. The goal was to bring out the detail and make the building look slightly weathered. I washed a little Khaki on the white parts, a little Grimy Black on the gray, and Concrete on the green and brown. See fig. 5.

Throughout construction, then, the general principle was to build a sub-assembly, then scrub it and apply a wash. After a wash in one color has dried, you can apply a second in some other. Just go easy — a little weathering goes a long way. We want our cement plant to look like a prosperous, well-maintained facility.

One other technique used was drybrushing, as described above. This was particularly effective for the roofs, which were painted black, left to dry thoroughly, then drybrushed with the Khaki to bring out the texture. Also the base was painted Concrete, then drybrushed with Khaki.

A LITTLE GREENERY

We haven't settled on a track plan, but the one here shows what we have so far. None of the track has been cemented down, so we can make changes easily.

Scenery is another area we haven't given much serious thought to, but why not plant a little grass, just to get away from our basic mud-flats look? The material we'll use is ground foam, which is simply latex foam rubber ground up and dyed. It's sold in plastic bags at hobby shops under several brand names.

Figure 6 shows how we applied tan latex paint with a small roller, then sprinkled on the foam. You can also brush on the paint, but the brush marks tend to be reflected in the finished landscape, giving a phony look. Vacuum lightly to remove excess foam.

Next month we'll assemble some special cars for hauling bulk cement to our cement plant, do a little detailing on the premises, and start switching cars. ☼

FIG. 6. SOME GRASS AND WEEDS
Left: We used a small paint roller to roll on flat tan latex. **Right:** While the paint was still wet we sprinkled on ground foam, using a fine-textured light green first and then a coarser grade. We avoided the golf-course look simply by letting plenty of the tan show through.

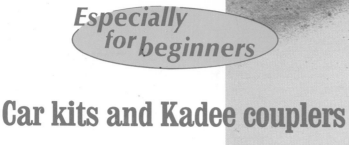

Car kits and Kadee couplers

Hey, we're starting to run this thing like a real railroad!

BY JIM KELLY

A. L. Schmidt

We spot a load of cement at the ready-mix plant. The Kadee couplers and magnetic uncoupling ramps add lots of fun to the layout. Two of our cars have been lightly weathered, using the same Polly S paints and techniques that we used on the cement plant last month.

LAST MONTH we built a cement plant for the HO railroad we introduced in the January issue. This month we've decided to build some covered hopper cars and start hauling cement. For easy coupling and uncoupling we'll equip our cars with Kadee couplers.

Cement is almost always carried in short covered hopper cars, usually two-bay types, sometimes three. The cars are short because cement is an extremely heavy commodity that would break the back of a fully loaded long car. And they're covered because if the train should run through a heavy rainstorm the railroad would have a big problem — worthless loads that are terribly difficult to get out of the cars!

Two of the cars we built are rounded-side types following a prototype built by American Car & Foundry (ACF). These are great lookers, but right now they are hard to find. Front Range was making them, but that company is no longer in business. Mine were by Accurail, and are Front Range cars this company bought to paint and sell under their own brand name.

The other three cars are by Model Die Casting, and you should be able to find these easily at your hobby shop. These represent Pullman-Standard cars built in the 1950s, many of which are still running.

Both of these kits fall into the easy-to-build category, although they aren't as easy — particularly for the beginner — as we're sometimes led to believe. Directions for the Accurail car, for example, say you can build it in 20 minutes. Sorry folks, but it took me about 1½ hours.

THE MDC CARS

I found the Model Die Casting cars easier to build, so let's do one of those first. Figure 1 shows what awaits you when you open the box. The first step is to clean up the cast-metal underframe as shown in fig. 2. After test-fitting to make sure it fits up in the body, wash it with soap and water, rinse it, and paint it black. I used the Polly S Grimy Black we bought for last month's projects.

I spent about an hour trying to fit the braces to the hoppers, as per the instructions for superdetailing, then gave up. My colleague, Jim Hediger, says the way to do it is to drill holes down through the hopper doorframes, insert the braces through them, cement them, then trim them off. Sounds good to me, and if I ever get back to it I'll try doing it that way. Meanwhile, the cars are running fine without the hopper details.

Clip parts carefully from the sprues, and file carefully so as to lose as little paint finish as possible. For the little cementing that's required, use a liquid cement for plastics, such as Testor's.

The most difficult part of an MDC kit is turning the self-tapping screws provided into the holes. It's easiest if you turn the screw in a few turns, back it out again to clear the threads, then give it another turn or so and clear it again. One hint: the smallest screws are for the trucks.

Tack the roof on with just a touch or two of glue, as you may want to add more weight later. The National Model Railroad Association recommends that cars this length weigh 3½ ounces. Both the MDC and Accurail cars are about an ounce light of that.

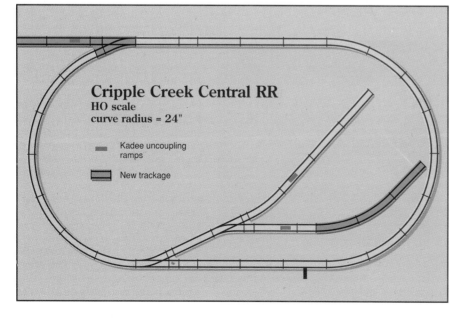

Cripple Creek Central RR
HO scale
curve radius = 24"

— Kadee uncoupling ramps

▭ New trackage

THE ACCURAIL CAR

Next we'll turn to the Accurail car. The parts are shown in fig. 3. The toughest part of building this car is getting it together without breaking off the corner steps. To help protect them I recommend you put the trucks on first, and this turns out to be a tricky operation. The truck-mounting holes for the plastic kingpins need to be enlarged by twirling carefully with a hobby knife, using a no. 11 blade. Keep twirling and checking until you have a snug fit, keeping the truck out of the way until you're actually ready to mount it.

Also, you'll find the kingpins are too long to hold the trucks down snug enough and need to be cut shorter. Cut at an angle, and you'll find it easier to get the kingpin started into the hole. The remainder of the car's construction requires some patience, but should give you no trouble.

I didn't want both my Rock Island ACF cars to have the same road number, so I modified one as shown in fig. 4. Later I learned that I could have saved myself the trouble, as Accurail also sells the car in a two-pack with two different road numbers.

After a little tinkering all five cars in my cement car fleet ran smoothly. The secret is adjusting the truck screws so that you have three-point suspension, as shown in fig. 5.

KADEE COUPLERS

Our Model Die Casting car kit includes the horn-hook couplers that come with most HO scale equipment. These neither look nor work much like real couplers, and so we're going to replace them with something much better, Kadee's Magne-Matic couplers.

When cars equipped with Kadees are spotted over a Kadee magnet, as shown at the beginning of this story, the knuckles are pulled to opposite sides and the cars uncouple. As long as you push smoothly you can shove a car a considerable distance beyond the magnet and drop it off.

Figure 6 shows the basic no. 5 coupler that will fit most HO equipment. Here we've installed it on a Mantua car.

The parts that come in Kadee's no. 5 kit are shown in fig. 7. For many HO cars you don't need the Kadee box, but can install the coupler directly into the box cast into the car's underframe. Such was the case with our cement cars and our locomotive. See fig. 8. Be aware of one potential problem, though. The metal coupler shank on our locomotive is grounded to the metal frame. This could cause electrical short circuits if we ever want to run this engine with another similarly equipped.

To convert our Mantua Heavyweights we simply removed the Mantua box and

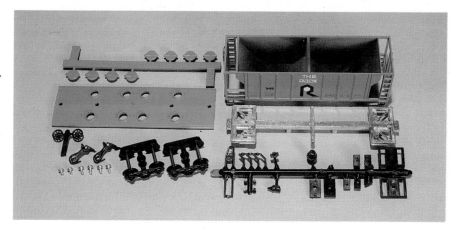

Products used

Accurail
1029 Rock Island two-bay hopper (2)
or 1030 set of two Rock Island hoppers with different numbers

Kadee
5 couplers (5)
231 Greas-em lubricant
321 uncoupling magnets (2)

Kato Unitrack
2-150 straight track sections (3)
2-220 24" curved sections
2-850 left-hand turnout

Mascot
855 screwdriver set

Model Die Casting
1431-1469, two-bay hoppers (5 of any road names you like)

Preiser
10036 standing truck drivers

X-acto
17 five-pack, no. 17 blades
3021 no. 1 hobby knife
73360 tweezers

Miscellaneous
Rubber cement
Small needlenose pliers
Small wood screws and washers
10" flat file, for metal only

Fig. 1. Here's what you'll find when you open a Model Die Casting twin-bay covered hopper kit. The most important feature is — drum roll — it comes already painted!

Fig. 2. The MDC underframe requires some cleaning up with a file. It's a good idea to buy a new flat file (say a 10") for this job and label it for use on metal only. It's hard to clean out all the metal particles that lodge in files, and they can scratch plastic badly.

Fig. 3. The Accurail car is a little tougher to build than the MDC car because it's difficult to make the truck kingpins fit. One nice feature is brass axles that won't be pulled into Kadee magnets the way steel ones are. The Front Range couplers included are nice, but don't couple with anything else.

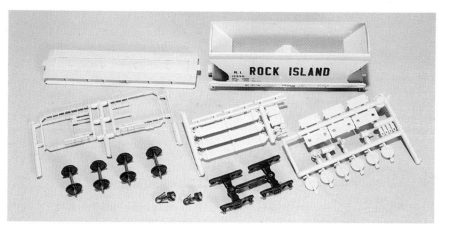

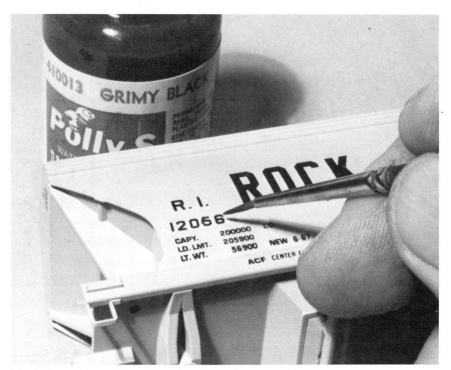

Fig. 4. Our author used a no. 0 brush to change the car number's last two digits from 56 to 68. On a lightly weathered car you can't tell the modification was made.

Fig. 6. Here's a Mantua Heavyweight boxcar equipped with a Kadee coupler. The Mantua coupler was replaced with Kadee's no. 5, attached with a Mantua screw.

ABOUT HO CARS

You'll find a tremendous variety of HO freight cars available at your hobby shop, everything from cars ready to run right out of the box to elaborate kits that will take dozens of hours to build.

Despite their convenience, ready-to-run cars generally are of inferior quality, with trucks and wheels that contribute to derailments. These are aimed at the inexpensive toy market, and the detail is usually heavy and crude.

The most popular cars among HO modelers, although we haven't used any yet for this project, are those made by Athearn. These are "shake-the-box" models that are about on the same difficulty level as Model Die Casting's.

Wm. K. Walthers and Eastern Car Works are among those offering plastic car kits that are more detailed. They have more parts and take longer to put together, though they're still easy.

At the far end of the difficulty spectrum are craftsman kits by Westerfield, Funaro & Camerlengo, and others. These are a challenge, but in the end offer great satisfaction.

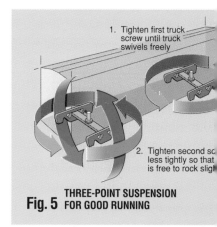

1. Tighten first truck screw until truck swivels freely

2. Tighten second sc less tightly so that is free to rock slig

Fig. 5 THREE-POINT SUSPENSION FOR GOOD RUNNING

lid and attached the Kadee box, using the Mantua screw. Figure 9 shows the easy method for removing the Kadee box parts from the sprue.

Follow the directions that come with the couplers, and they'll work great. It's especially important to smooth any rough surfaces as you go along and to use Kadee's Greas-em, a powdered lubricant.

We cemented the magnets to our track with rubber cement, as shown in fig. 10. This will hold them just fine, yet if you change your mind on location you can pull them off easily and place them elsewhere. Just rub the dried cement off with your thumb.

OPERATIONS

We added some new track this month, as shown on the track plan, including an interchange track that links our little railroad with the rest of the world. See fig. 11.

Already we're able to do more than just run around in circles. To start, we can haul cement from our interchange track, where it's left off by a neighboring railroad, to the cement plant. Once there we have to spot our caboose on the station track, pull out the empty cement cars and spot them ahead of the caboose, then shove the loads into the

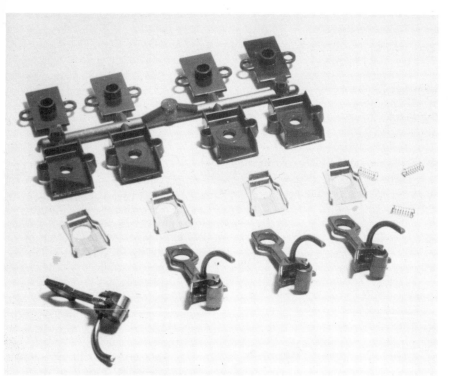

Fig. 10. Rubber cement worked fine for attaching Kadee magnets to our Unitrack. The magnets project a bit above the railhead, but we've decided we can live with that and don't want to cut into the track.

Fig. 7. Inside the Kadee no. 5 envelope you'll find these parts. From top to bottom are the mounting boxes, centering springs, and couplers. On the right are spare knuckle springs.

Fig. 8. Left: To install Kadee couplers in our Atlas S-2, we pulled the coupler box pin.
Right: We positioned the Kadee centering spring and coupler, then put the box back on.

Fig. 9. Below: It's easy to remove the Kadee parts from the sprue, using a no. 17 chisel blade. Many modelers keep two hobby knives, one with a no. 11 blade and another with a no. 17.

plant. Meanwhile, we may have a boxcar with LCL (less-than-carload) freight for the station and some other cars to spot beyond the station for off-loading to trucks.

Then it's time to head back for the interchange with our empties. As soon as we get them there we can just let them sit until later, when we can imagine that they've gone on and returned, or we can actually take them off the layout and replace them with others. Using this latter concept, we can easily justify a fleet of a half-dozen or more cement cars. Eastern Car Works has some really neat — albeit a little more difficult — hopper car kits that you'd now enjoy.

Have you noticed that the poor guys working down at the cement plant are missing some vital ingredients? Next month we're going to solve their problem by adding a sand and gravel spur. See you then. ◊

Fig. 11. Our interchange track leads to that great world beyond our layout, so we used our razor saw to cut a notch in the wood trim to accommodate it. That "invisible" rail bumper is made from the box our Preiser figures came in. Just rough-cut it with the razor saw, then file it to the finished shape. Attach it with some nice, small screws so you don't split the wood as our author did.

17

was to "stain" the gray a dark brown and give it the look of weathered wood rather then just painting it a solid color.

I used the same technique but Polly S Weathered Black on the plastic rail section, with surprisingly effective results. For gray plastic it sure looks a lot like a piece of railroad track. Some washed-on black on the ramp also made the cast-in gravel look more real.

ASSEMBLING THE CARS

While my paint was drying I assembled several of the automatic-dumping hopper cars, following the directions.

Last month we were lucky in having no problems with installing Kadee couplers on our cars, but not so this time. When I installed the couplers in the Con-Cor boxes, they came out too high and needed to be shimmed down.

As shown in fig. 1, I lowered the top of the built-in boxes by filing the Con-Cor box covers until they fit into the boxes, then cemented them in.

Next, as shown in fig. 2, I assembled the Kadee couplers in their own boxes and mounted them with screws. To do this you'll need a pin vise (a tool for holding drill bits), a no. 50 bit, and a tap for a no. 2-72 screw.

Drilling and tapping holes may be something new for you and may seem a bit intimidating. But it's easy (and fun) and is the only really right way to mount the couplers in this situation. If you just glue them they probably won't stand up to the repeated stress of banging

Especially for beginners

A. L. Schmidt

Adding an operating gravel dumper

Paint and scenery make this toy-like accessory look good

BY JIM KELLY

THIS MONTH we'll add to the operating fun on our HO scale beginner's layout by installing a gravel dock at the cement plant, using Con-Cor's no. 6100 operating ramp/hopper set. (The same kit is offered by Heljan.)

Like many model railroading projects, this one began as an exercise in painting. Built straight from the box, this would be a toy-like affair indeed, but some simple painting techniques make it look just fine.

To get started I cut all the parts from the sprues carefully, using a hobby knife, then I trimmed off flash with a hobby knife and a large, flat file. To kill the plastic shine and provide a base for further painting I spray-painted all the parts lightly with a can of Floquil's gray primer. In our shop we use a spray booth equipped with an exhaust fan, but most of you won't have such equipment and should do this job outdoors. Floquil is a solvent-based paint and inhaling the fumes can be harmful.

After the primer had dried 24 hours, I brushed a wash coat of Polly S Roof Brown over the wood deck parts. Basically this was a matter of brushing on some brown, then dipping the brush in water and brushing some more. The idea

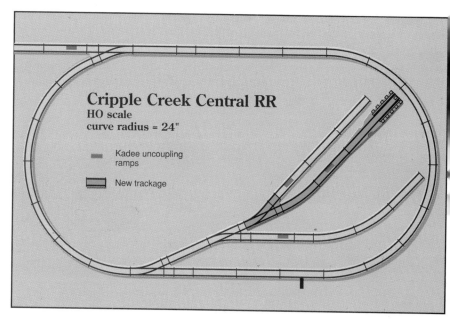

Cripple Creek Central RR
HO scale
curve radius = 24"

▬ Kadee uncoupling ramps

▭ New trackage

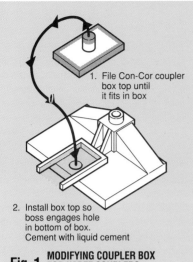

1. File Con-Cor coupler box top until it fits in box

2. Install box top so boss engages hole in bottom of box. Cement with liquid cement

Fig. 1 MODIFYING COUPLER BOX FOR KADEE COUPLERS

into the bumping post on the ramp — and you'll find bumping that post helps a lot in getting the hopper doors to open and dump properly.

And speaking of those doors, I found mine worked best if I stretched and weakened the springs as shown in fig. 3. At full strength the springs exert so much pressure that the switch engine can't shove the cars hard enough to depress them and open the doors. Also the cars tend to derail on the dock if the springs are full-strength.

PLACING THE RAMP

Look at the track plan, and you'll notice that we've added a new turnout as well as a siding this month. The track leading to our ramp is Kato's Unitrack,

but on the ramp itself we used Atlas sectional track.

Figure 4 shows how we had to saw the tail off the ramp to fit it to the Unitrack. This was necessary because the ramp is designed to take a track coming directly off the tabletop, with no roadbed.

Sawing the tail off the track meant I had to shorten one of two Atlas track sections, a job done with the razor saw. I used Atlas rail joiners to fit the Atlas track to the Kato. You need to pinch them a bit with needlenose pliers after sliding them on to get a good connection.

The kit comes with a plastic tray that slides in under the dock, the idea being that the car dumps gravel into the tray, then you pull the tray out and dump it somewhere — probably just back into the car.

Since our foam layout is so easy to cut into, I decided to improve on this feature by installing a funnel under the dock, as shown in fig. 5. The funnel (about 3″ in diameter) was one in a set of three bought at Target for about $1.

I hid the funnel by building up some mounding around the hole, using a product called Sculptamold. More and more hobby shops are carrying it, but if yours doesn't try an art supply store or craft shop. Sculptamold is the most mess-free material we've found for building scenery, and we recommend it highly. Just add a little water and mix it into a stiff batter. It goes where you put it, with none of the dripping and mess of plaster. Later in this series, when we build some scenery, we'll be using it again.

After the Sculptamold had set (you don't have to wait for it to dry, which

ABOUT CLEANING TRACK

The Achilles heel of model railroading is that tiny footprint where metal wheel meets metal rail. Let some dirt and gunk get in the way, and eventually your locomotive will begin running jerkily and stalling. We need to keep those "juices flowing" by maintaining good electrical contact between the rails and the wheels, and that means keeping the rails clean.

Lots of liquid track cleaners are available at hobby shops, but abrasive cleaning pads remain one of the easiest and best ways to clean rail. These pads are about the size and consistency of ink erasers. Of the several brands available at hobby shops, Bright Boy is one of the best known.

may take several days), I painted it heavily with Polly S Concrete left over from one of our earlier projects and sprinkled on gravel, letting the paint act as an adhesive.

So far we haven't glued any track down, but for the ramp it was imperative. The adhesive I used was Walthers Goo. This is a rubber-based cement you'll find extremely handy for bonding dissimilar materials (here plastic and latex paint). Just run a bead of Goo on the bottom edges of the ramp, wait about a minute, then place it in position. I put several books on the ramp

FIG. 2. INSTALLING KADEE COUPLERS
Left: Utilizing the Kadee box lid as a drill guide, we drilled the floor with a no. 50 bit. Then we tapped it for a no. 2-56 screw.
Above: The coupler, mounted in its box, is screwed to the floor.

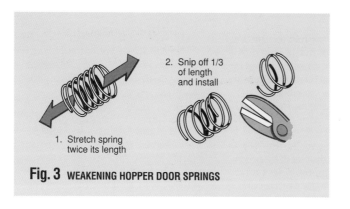

Fig. 3 WEAKENING HOPPER DOOR SPRINGS

1. Stretch spring twice its length
2. Snip off 1/3 of length and install

Fig. 4. Right: To make the height of our ramp track match the Unitrack lead, we had to cut off the tail. We removed 4⅜", which proved to be too much. Cutting off 3" would be about right. You could then use an Atlas 6" straight and not have to cut any track.

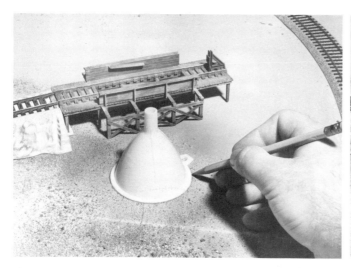

FIG. 5. DISAPPEARING GRAVEL TRICK
Left: Once satisfied with the location of the ramp, we moved it aside and marked the location for our plastic funnel. **Middle:** We cut a eled hole with a hobby knife and then cemented the funnel in pos

FIG. 6. FINISHING THE RAMP
Left: Before cementing the ramp down we cleaned away the scenery material with a putty knife. **Above:** Our next step was to cemen ramp in position with Goo, using heavy books to weight it d

for about an hour so the Goo could really set up. See fig. 6.

BALLAST AND SCENERY

Hmmm, you may be saying, the track on that ramp needs something. Right you are, and what it needs is ballast. I used Life-Like's Scene Masters, which several experiments also revealed was the best material for hauling in the hopper cars because it flowed out best.

Using a plastic cup as a dispenser, I distributed the ballast on the track, then smoothed it out with a flat brush. (Tapping lightly on the rails also helps smooth the ballast.) Then I diluted yellow glue about 4:1 with water, added a drop of dishwashing detergent, and used an eyedropper to apply it to the ballast.

After 24 hours the ballast will be

ove: We used Sculptamold to mound up und the edges of the funnel and hide it.

glued in place, but will look as if it's lying there loosely. (Incidentally, you have now mastered one variation of what's called the "bonded ballast method.")

The plastic rocks cast into the ramp look phony, so we virtually eliminated them by painting the rock areas with tan latex paint, then sprinkling on various shades of ground foam scenery material. Although we were using the paint as an adhesive, we also applied a little diluted yellow glue with the eyedropper to hold some of our larger "weeds" in place.

RESULTS

How well does the ramp work? you might ask. Not perfect, but better than I had expected. Sometimes a door will need a nudge with a pencil point to open. Also, only about two-thirds of the contents will flow out. Light tapping on the car with a pencil will get most of the rest out.

I added a little Johnson's Baby Powder to the ballast, which seemed to improve the flow slightly, and if nothing else, made it smell nice. If you try this, use only a little or you'll be getting a lot of dust on the rails.

The ballast falling through the dock is collected in a small plastic pitcher, also bought at Target. I twirled holes in the sides and put on a bail made from picture-frame wire. This hangs from a sheet-metal screw turned into one of the foam core joists. Eventually I may have a gravel pit somewhere on the road where I can dump the gravel into a tipple and use it to load cars.

Next time we're going to do a simple project, adding a road to the layout. Hope to see you then. ⬡

Products used

Amaco
Sculptamold (3-pound bag)

Atlas
150 straight 9″ track sections, 2 (or substitute one no. 822 6″ section for one 9″ straight)

Con-Cor
6100 ramp/hopper car set
6101-6107 operating hopper cars, use any 2 road names

Floquil
130009 Primer Spray, 1 can

Kadee
5 couplers (2 pks)
205 coupler height gauge

Kato Unitrack
EP550-L left-hand turnout
S246 straight section

Life-Like
Scene Masters gray ballast (1 bag)

Mascot
811 pin vise

Walthers
no. 50 drill bit
299 Goo (1 tube)
1304 2-56 tap

Woodland Scenics
834 Hob-Bits ¼″ 2-56 screws (2 pks)

Miscellaneous
Bright Boy track cleaner
pipette (eyedropper)
plastic funnel (3″ diameter)
plastic pitcher

ft: Because we cut the ramp too short, we had to shim the end of the track with cardboard. We blended the ramp track and Unitrack together with Sculptamold. **Above:** We added ballast to the ramp track, then bonded it with dilute yellow glue applied with an eyedropper.

A road for your layout

Foam core board makes an excellent base material

BY JIM KELLY

ROADS are important details on a small railroad like our HO scale Cripple Creek Central because they broaden its horizons. These highways and byways can slash across the layout dramatically, or they can wander around and through scenic features. Either way, they help divert our attention from the basic loop of track and contribute to the illusion that there's a world out there beyond the layout's edge.

Modelers have discovered lots of good ways to make roads — the materials or techniques aren't as important as a few basic design and construction principles, to wit:

• Model roads should be elevated above the surrounding terrain because

real roads are. Those that aren't become thoroughfares for boats when heavy rains come. Ideally roads should have ditches, but that's asking a bit much on a small beginner's layout.

• A model road should be smooth. Keep in mind that in HO a ⅛″ depression is a foot-deep pothole. Also, as man-made objects, roads should generally be smoother and straighter than natural objects. Part of the art of model railroading comes in playing on the contrast between what's natural and what's artificial, perhaps even exaggerating it.

I've said little in this series about planning, largely because I haven't had a plan, only a general notion of where the layout is going. Figure 1, though, shows a little study that went into deciding where to place the road on the layout. My colleagues agreed with my choice. See if you do too. The 2⅜″-wide strips of ¹⁄₁₆″-thick gray mounting board I cut for this study turned out to be the surface of the road.

GETTING STARTED

So far none of the track had been glued down, but now seemed the time to do so with part of it, as indicated on the track plan. For this job I used Walthers Goo, working three track sections at a time. I'd run a bead along each bottom edge, let it set for about a minute, then put the track in position and push down.

Since this was to be a fairly important road through the heart of a town, I wanted it to be elevated several feet above the table surface. The material chosen was ³⁄₁₆″-thick foam core board, the same material used to make the layout table in the January issue (except that then we used ½″-thick material.)

Cripple Creek Central RR
HO scale
curve radius = 24″

▬ 3/16″ foam core board

▭ Track glued down

FIG. 1. PLANNING THE ROAD

Above: At first we thought that we would run the road in front of a series of stores. The scene was mocked up using buildings from another layout and strips of illustration board.
Below: We liked this arrangement better, even though we'll be looking at the stores from behind. It opens up the view of the gravel ramp we built last month. Besides, the street scene should be especially interesting when viewed from the right end of the layout.

Products used

Amaco
Sculptamold (3-pound bag)

Floquil paint
110132 SP *Lark* Dark Gray

General
1251 scale rule

Highball ballast
10 Dirt
124 Cinders (N scale)

Northeastern
181 1/16″ x 5/64″ stripwood, 24″ long (2)

Polly S paint
410013 Grimy Black
410070 Roof Brown

Preiser
0027 seated figures
0118 standing figures
3200 Suzuki 4-wheeler with figures

Railway Models
SS0401 plastic brick sheet

Sequoia
2005 wheel stops

Woodland Scenics
49 blended turf, mixed
63 coarse turf, light green
65 coarse turf, dark green

Miscellaneous
colored pencil, white
colored pencil, yellow
latex paint, flat tan (1 quart)
putty knife
yellow glue
20″ x 30″ foam core board, 3/16″ thick
20″ x 30″ mounting board, heavy

Foam core board is nothing more than a slice of expanded plastic foam laminated between two sheets of heavy paper. It's light, strong, and very easy to cut, making it an ideal material for building up bases for structures, roads, parking lots, and so forth. You can cut it easily with a hobby or utility knife.

I decided to make the road 22 feet wide. Actual roads are usually wider, but in model railroading, particularly on small layouts, we often model the nonrailroad features a bit undersize.

To get started I cut a few 2⅜″-wide (22 scale feet) foam core strips. I laid these on the layout and cut them off where they butted against the base of the track. Figure 2 shows how I made a pattern for the one curved piece needed. As soon as this piece was cut, I used it as a template to mark the roadway surface on the illustration board, allowing some extra length on the end that butted against the ends of the ties, to be trimmed off later.

Our station was setting in a hole between the tracks, so while I was in a foam core cutting mood I also cut a base for the station and a parking area, as shown in the track plan.

Figure 3 shows how I bulldozed the route with a scraper before gluing the form core strips in place with yellow glue. I piled on books and other weights to hold the road base down until the glue had set. Yellow glue was used again to fasten the cardboard surface to the foam core board, with lots of weight added, as the cardboard tends to curl up at the edges.

PAINTING AND DETAILS

I used Sculptamold to model the edges of the road. This is a fiber and plaster product that's much easier to control and neater to work with than regular plaster. You'll find it in some hobby and craft shops and in artist's supply stores.

My original plan was to apply the Sculptamold so neatly that I wouldn't have to paint the cardboard, but — alas and alack — it was not to be. The

FIG. 2. LAYING THE FOAM-CORE ROAD BASE
Left: The foam-core roadbed strips were marked and cut to fit against the base of our Kato Unitrack. These strips will raise the road above the terrain. **Middle:** To make a curve we drew a pattern on paper, cut it out, and transferred it to the foam core board. **Right:** We used the curved section to mark and cut the straight.

color I used was Floquil's Southern Pacific *Lark* Dark Gray, about right for asphalt. (Look around, and you'll notice that blacktop roads aren't black — they're shades of gray.)

Sculptamold may take several days to dry in an application like this, but you don't need to wait before proceeding with scenery application. After the Sculptamold had set firm (about an hour), I painted the shoulders of the road with flat tan latex paint, working quickly and in small areas so the surface would still be plenty wet when I started added scenery texturing materials.

First I added a little Highball Dirt, then I sprinkled on ground foam, starting

with Woodland Scenics mixed turf and adding a bit of coarse dark green. The secret of good-looking ground cover on a model railroad is using a variety of materials and not sprinkling them on too heavily or too evenly. You want the brown ground to show through here and there. You can always add more scenery material, but taking off excess is more difficult — usually you just have to paint the area tan again and start over.

The wet latex paint will bond much of the scenery material in place, but for extra insurance I dribbled on yellow glue, diluted about 4 to 1 with water, using an eyedropper. A drop or two of dishwashing detergent mixed in will

cause this adhesive to seep nicely into the scenery and disappear.

PARKING LOTS

I was planning an asphalt parking lot for the station, but at the last minute decided to go with the plastic brick material, cementing it to the foam core with Goo. To add mortar I painted on Polly S Brown, then wiped it off the brick surfaces with a paper towel. What a nice little spot of color and interest this added to the layout! Variety may or may not be the spice of life, but it's definitely the spice of model railroading.

Across the road from the station I

ABOUT SCALE RULES

As beginners, we usually leave it to the manufacturers to make sure the equipment and kits we buy are properly proportioned. Eventually, though, we'll want to build something like a road or a building from scratch, and we'll want to make sure it's in scale.

One way to do that is to take the prototype dimension in inches and divide it by the scale factor, 87.1 in the case of HO. This is easily done in our age of electronic calculators.

Much handier, though, is a scale rule, like the one on the edge of this page. This is similar to the rulers we're all familiar with, except that the markings are in scale feet and inches. A rule with markings for a variety of model railroad scales is best because you can use it to take measurements off a plan drawn in one scale and transfer them to your modeling material in another.

FIG. 4. LITTLE THINGS MEAN A LOT
At the station we used timber road crossings. We stained the wood strips with Poll Brown thinned with water, let them dry overnight, and cut them to length. With hea wood like this you have to cut into the wood and snap it, making it slightly longer than quired, then trim or sand the ends. In the coming months we'll add the crossing ga

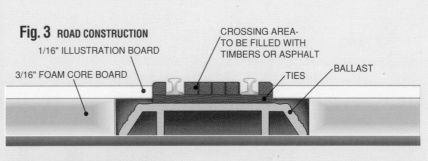

Fig. 3 ROAD CONSTRUCTION

1/16" ILLUSTRATION BOARD

3/16" FOAM CORE BOARD

CROSSING AREA- TO BE FILLED WITH TIMBERS OR ASPHALT

TIES

BALLAST

FIG. 3. COMPLETING THE ROAD
Left: We bulldozed scenery material from the roadway so our yellow glue would stick well. **Below left:** The road shoulders were formed with Sculptamold. **Below:** To model an asphalt grade crossing we mixed Polly S Grimy Black paint with thick Sculptamold.

built up the area with foam core board and Sculptamold to build another parking lot and an area for unloading railroad cars spotted on our team track (so called because in the early days such unloading areas were served by wagons and teams of horses). Opting for variety again, I painted this area with tan latex, then sprinkled on Highball's cinders.

GRADE CROSSINGS

Figure 4 shows the two kinds of grade crossings I installed. Timber crossings are seldom seen nowadays, but they always look attractive. The asphalt crossing is actually more typical.

The final detail was lines on the road, drawn with colored pencils available at

artist's supply stores. You need to blunt the points so as to make lines about a scale 6" wide. Test on a scrap piece of cardboard before drawing.

Next month master modeler Art Curren will add a store to the layout. He's making it especially to fit that triangular lot kitty-corner from the station. You're going to like it! ⟡

our asphalt crossing we mixed Polly S Grimy Black with Sculptamold and ap-
d it with a putty knife, making sure to clear the flangeways. This works better
trying to take the cardboard right up to the rail, which invariably leads to a
er sticking up and derailments. This same colored Sculptamold was used to
el the transition from the street to the brick parking lot at the station.

To keep cars out of streets and yards, a bumper is usually located at the end of each siding. It may be a simple pile of gravel, a wood or rail post, a tie bolted across the track, or a more elaborate affair made by welding rails together. Railroads also buy ready-made bumpers, including some like these HO scale wheel stops by Sequoia. Kato sells a track end piece, but we just piled ballast and sprinkled on ground foam.

By combining two plastic kits our author created this "mom and pop" bike store that looks right at home on our HO layout.

Clyde's Cycle Center

Your introduction to the art of kitbashing

BY ART CURREN
PHOTOS BY A. L. SCHMIDT

CLYDE'S CYCLE CENTER is the first of a series of buildings that will front on the road we built last month. It's a small shop added to an existing house — a common sight all over this nation.

This will be a simple kitbashing project. We're going to build a unique structure by combining (or "bashing") buildings from two HO scale structure kits, a house manufactured by Model Power and a corner store by Tyco.

THE ORIGINAL HOUSE

The house is typical of frame houses found everywhere and is nicely proportioned, cleverly designed, and easy to assemble. I followed the sequence assembly given in the directions, but made some additions and changes.

To cement the structures together I used liquid plastic cement, applied with an artist's brush. This softens the surfaces just enough to bond them together. Before bonding a joint, check it for a good fit and correct any problems with a hobby knife or small file.

I added some square plastic bracing in the corners, as shown in fig. 1. These add strength in critical joints and help with squareness. They came from Evergreen, which makes styrene strips and sheet in a wide range of sizes.

The Model Power instructions are good, but one important detail not covered is that you *must* cement the roofs together before adding the smaller wing. The wing has to fit under the roof to be correctly located.

Another thing I found was that both chimneys have the same angle at the bottom, but that the roof angles are different. One chimney will have to be filed at a different angle to fit the larger roof.

Speaking of chimneys, the paint on the surfaces to be joined must be scraped or filed off; otherwise, the bond

Fig. 1. Our author adds bracing (square styrene strip) to corners. The view block, cut from black construction paper, prevents us from looking in one window and straight out the others. You can see how shades and curtains are painted on the back of the window glass.

CLYDE'S CYCLE CENTER

CLYDE'S BICYCLES

BICYCLES
SALES•SERVICE

BIKES

HO SCALE

will be weak. (The sprues containing the chimneys and the porch roofs are molded gray, but these parts have been painted red.)

MAKING CHANGES

You don't have to make most of the changes I did, but they're fun and will help distinguish your model from a structure built straight from the box.

With a few extra windows at our disposal (including three we gain by not using any on the walls where the addition will go), we can enhance our building with windows on the peaks.

The large peaks get the large windows, and the small window goes on the wing. To make window openings I usually drill a hole in the center and enlarge it by twirling a hobby knife, as shown in fig. 2. When the hole is large enough I start carving excess plastic away, alternating my strokes as if I were chopping with an ax. As the hole nears the final size, I finish up the opening with a small file.

Doors C5 and C6 may be placed in any window opening you choose. This bonus lets us move the big porch over to the side and the small one to the rear. For the rear porch, I added diagonal support braces made from .040″-square styrene.

For the sake of variety I converted my foundation from stone to brick by cementing on plastic brick material. Also, I added cellar windows and a cellar door, as shown in fig. 3.

Figure 4 shows how I added a cap and flue pipe to each chimney.

FINISHING TOUCHES

After assembling the model I sprayed the walls with Testor's Dullcote. This is a flat, clear finish that makes the model look more realistic by killing the raw plastic shine.

I glazed the windows with clear styrene from the Tyco kit, as I like it better than the acetate Model Power provides. Shades and curtains are simply painted on from behind.

To add mortar to the chimneys and foundation I painted on Pactra White, then wiped it off, leaving paint in the joints. To accentuate the roof shingles

Art changed the appearance of his Model Power house by adding windows to the roof peaks.

you can flow on a wash of Polly S Grimy Black. I painted the undersides and edges of the roofs with Floquil White.

THE BIKE SHOP

This addition is designed to fit the triangular corner where the road and

the railroad tracks meet. To help in planning I made a paper template of the lot's shape.

Flip the kit roof piece over, and use the template in fig. 5 to cut the new roof from it. Then assemble the walls around the new roof, using the corner

That fence helps keep kids off the railroad track. The cellar door is just inside the nearest gate.

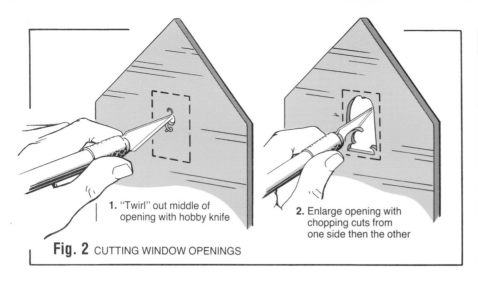

Fig. 2 CUTTING WINDOW OPENINGS

1. "Twirl" out middle of opening with hobby knife

2. Enlarge opening with chopping cuts from one side then the other

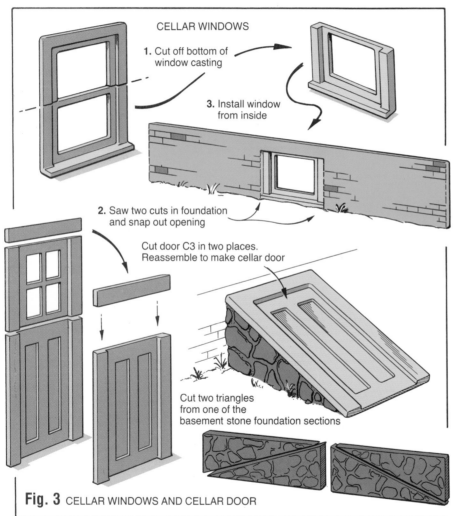

CELLAR WINDOWS

1. Cut off bottom of window casting

3. Install window from inside

2. Saw two cuts in foundation and snap out opening

Cut door C3 in two places. Reassemble to make cellar door

Cut two triangles from one of the basement stone foundation sections

Fig. 3 CELLAR WINDOWS AND CELLAR DOOR

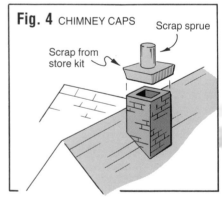

Fig. 4 CHIMNEY CAPS

Scrap sprue

Scrap from store kit

entrance wall and the two end walls. I filed the mating corners a little to make them fit better in their new relationships to one another.

Using a razor saw I cut a portion from the kit's rear wall to become the short end wall next to the large part of the house. I could have cut the other short wall needed from the same piece, but decided to get fancy and suggest that the building was made of concrete

block with a stone veneer. To show this I used a small piece of Pikestuff concrete block material as well as a small tile cap, also from Pikestuff.

The wall capping on the rest of the building is Evergreen 4" x 10" HO strip. I added mortar to the stones, using the procedure already mentioned. Then I installed roof vents from the Tyco kit. Finally, I painted the roof with Grimy Black to represent tar.

THE BIKES

My four unmanned bikes came from the NJ International Crowd Pleasers playground kit. Also included were a bike rack, swing, seesaw, and slide. These details are molded in silver plastic, so some painting is required. I also used some Preiser bikes with riders.

Nice as they are, the NJ International bikes have no handlebars. To

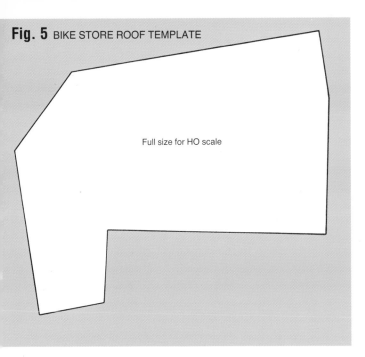

Fig. 5 BIKE STORE ROOF TEMPLATE

Full size for HO scale

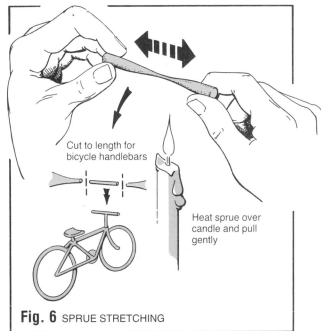

Cut to length for bicycle handlebars

Heat sprue over candle and pull gently

Fig. 6 SPRUE STRETCHING

remedy this, I'll introduce you to a new skill — sprue-stretching. To create longer handlebars, I took a section of the silver sprue and held it over a candle flame until the plastic began to soften. Then I pulled it to create a thin bar, as shown in fig. 6. This bar was cut up to make handlebars.

THE BASE

Figure 7 shows how I modified the house base and scribed in a sidewalk, complete with cracks. I painted the walks with Floquil Antique White.

I cemented the base/sidewalk to a base cut from $3/16''$-thick foam core, then filled in the lawn areas with pieces of green felt. You can tease the felt with a brass-bristle, suede-shoe brush to make some of the fibers stand up. Don't forget the bare dirt spot underneath each swing.

Once the building was finished, we cemented it to the layout with Walthers Goo, pinning it down with nails until the cement could set. Then we worked it in around the edges with Sculptamold, the plaster-like scenery product we've been using.

Woodland Scenics ground foam sprinkled over wet tan latex paint gave us some ground cover. White glue, diluted with water, was applied with an eyedropper to bond the scenery materials in place. Some weeds were made using small lengths of green yarn.

And there you have it, an introduction to the art of kitbashing. It's not so much a way of modeling, as it is a way of thinking. With practice you can learn to look at kits and see worlds of possibilities for modifying and changing them to make the model you want and need. ☼

ABOUT KITBASHING

This term describes the art of modifying and rearranging the parts of one or more kits to make a unique model. Kitbashing is an alternative to building a model completely from scratch.

Kitbashing (or "kitmingling," as I like to call it because the term sounds so much gentler) can be very simple. An example would be moving the porches to different walls, as we've done with the house portion of Clyde's Cycle Center. Alterations can also be more complex, as we did with the drugstore to wed it to the house.

Kitmingling amounts to creating your own kits by combining pieces from kits in new ways. It's fun, challenging, and rewarding as you build something that's exclusively your own.

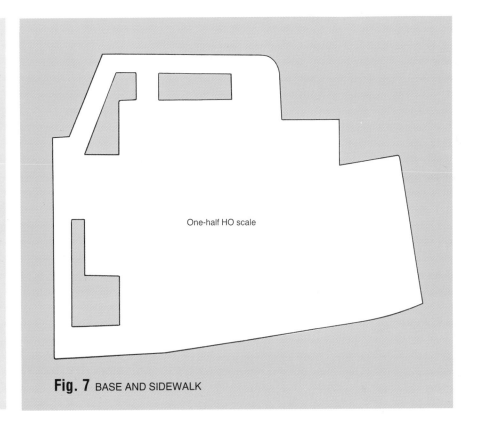

One-half HO scale

Fig. 7 BASE AND SIDEWALK

A blue sky and paper backdrop buildings add a world beyond our HO Cripple Creek Central.

Color photos by Chris Becker

Adding a backdrop

An easy way to make a small layout look larger

BY JIM KELLY

HOW DO YOU make a small layout look larger? Lots of scenery tricks can help, but one of the niftiest ploys is to add a backdrop that divides the layout into separate areas. The backdrop helps you direct the viewer's attention where you want it to go, and also allows you

more freedom in creating scenery. As shown in fig. 1, what's on one side of the backdrop doesn't have to line up with or match what's on the other side. (Eventually I plan to take advantage of this feature and build some hilly scenery on the far side of the layout.)

The backdrop I made for this project weighs practically nothing and can be

simply lifted off. It's made of foam-core board, some cardboard, and a few sticks.

MAKING THE SKYBOARD

Step one was to cut a piece of $^3/_{16}$″ foam-core board 14″ x 52$^3/_4$″. This material, in case you haven't tried it, is a slice of plastic foam sandwiched between two sheets of heavy paper. You can buy it at art supply stores, which sometimes will cut it to your specifications.

To cut the foam-core board yourself, all you need are a straightedge and a sharp utility or hobby knife. Use several light cuts, rather than one heavy one that may easily wander off line.

Next I painted the sky blue. On my first attempt I made the mistake of applying the paint heavily with a roller and trying to do both sides at once. As the foam core dried, it curled to where I could no longer use it. On the second attempt I brushed on the paint, heavily enough to cover, but not enough to cause curling. I painted one side, let it dry for three hours on a flat surface, then turned it over and painted the other.

While the paint was drying, I cemented the backdrop mounting strip to the layout (fig. 2). This is $^1/_2$″ x $^3/_4$″ wood sash trim, which I bought at Menards, a builder's supply store. I would think the large home supply stores or lumberyards in your area would have it. You can cut this wood easily with a hobby razor saw. Our strip is 51$^1/_4$″ long.

Fig. 1. Our backdrop lifts off easily, so we won't wreck it by building scenery. In future episodes we'll add some hills on the back side.

Fig. 2. We cemented a strip of 1/2″ x 3/4″ wood to the layout, with the narrow side down, then weighted it until the yellow glue had set. The finished backdrop clips over this wood strip.

FIG. 3. PAPER BACKDROP BUILDINGS

Above: Instant Horizons backdrops are simply paintings of buildings or rural scenery printed on sheets of paper. **Right:** We cemented the backdrops to black mounting board, then cut out the sky, removing most rooftop detail at the same time. We also trimmed away the skyscrapers on our city section to get the look of a smaller city.

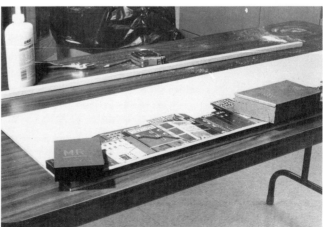

FIG. 4. ASSEMBLING THE BACKDROP

Above: We used more of the 1/2″ x 3/4″ wood strip material to space the buildings out from the backdrop. Note that the strip across the bottom had to be up 3/4″ to make room for the wood strip that's cemented to the layout (see fig. 2). We painted the narrow sides of the strips flat black before cutting them to length and gluing them in place. **Right:** The buildings, now mounted on the black mounting board, were cemented to the wood strips and weighted down until the cement had set.

31

PAPER BACKDROPS

The backdrop buildings were bought at the hobby shop and are simply printed on sheets of paper. See fig. 3.

Instant Horizons has about a dozen scenes available in its line, and paper backdrops are also available from Detail Associates and MZZ. You can just cement these backdrops to the foam core, but I prefer to cut away the sky — for my tastes it's too light a shade of blue and too shiny. Besides, I wanted to explore the three-dimensional effect I'd get by mounting the flat backdrop buildings out in front of the backdrop just a fraction of an inch.

With scissors, I cut away most of the sky. Then I mounted my paper backdrops on black mounting board, using 3M Photo Mount in a ten-ounce spray can and following the directions on the can. Both the mounting board and the Photo Mount are available at artist's supply stores. You spray the back of the paper, then the cardboard, wait a few minutes, and join them together.

Do make sure to use black mounting board for this if you can find it, because the cut black edge looks really classy on the cut-out buildings.

Next comes the hard part, cutting out the buildings. Use a straightedge and a hobby knife equipped with a sharp no. 11 blade. Change blades frequently. Compare the finished backdrop with the paper version, shown in fig. 1, and you'll see that most of the roof details were cut away. All those water towers and chimneys would be too hard to cut around and could easily be damaged later.

Figure 4 shows how the backdrop was finished, using more of the trim wood as spacers. Much to my surprise and joy, it fit perfectly over the strip I'd glued to the layout. The 3-D effect worked out great, and I like this much better than a backdrop with the paper buildings glued directly to it.

Make sure to join us next month when the old pro, Gordon Odegard, adds a pond to the layout. ⌀

A stream and a lake for the Cripple Creek

Adding water is easy on this HO layout

BY GORDON ODEGARD
PHOTOS BY THE AUTHOR

Color photos by A. L. Schmidt

Maybe you hadn't noticed it, but our small HO scale layout is named the Cripple Creek Central. So, to paraphrase a Wendy's ad from a few years back, "Where's the creek?" The creek — and a lake — are what this article's all about.

With a sophisticated layout that's constructed with girders, risers, stringers, and such, it's not difficult to build in lakes and water courses of various sizes and depths. It's another matter altogether with a flat tabletop, especially one made of plywood. But as you know, we were thinking ahead. Foam core is easy to cut holes in! No drilling, no saber saws — just a sharp knife. So get out your utility knife with a new blade, and let's get to work.

CUTTING OUT THE LAKE

My first step was to draw a template (fig. 1) of the shape and size I thought appropriate. I next positioned the drawing on the layout and cut right through it with my hobby knife. The only things I had to be careful of were the stringers beneath the layout.

You can see in fig. 1 that I brutally cut right through the tabletop for the lake. For Cripple Creek I sliced only part way through, gouging deeper and deeper with a sharp chisel as I approached the tracks and lake. I didn't remove the foam core beneath the tracks, but I widened out the stream and lake where the culvert would be placed.

Once the lake and stream edges had been defined, I used the knife to cut in banks (shown in fig. 2) at about a 45-degree angle. With this done, I cut pieces of 1/4" foam core to serve as the lake bed and parts of the streambed I had cut through. I used yellow carpenter's glue to secure these in place as

tightly and completely as I could so our "water" wouldn't leak out. I let this dry a day or two until it had firmly set.

SCULPTAMOLD GROUND

Foam core is a wonderful product, but it doesn't look much like terra firma. It's smooth, and we want bumpy. To make our layout look bumpy, I picked up a bag of Sculptamold. Any good artist's supply store and some craft shops carry small (3-pound) plastic bags. For this project I used maybe half a bag.

I started by filling an old or disposable cup about half full of water. Then I mixed in Sculptamold until the mixture got thick and pasty. At this point, I

scooped out part of the goop and, with a small palette knife, I spread it along the lake and stream banks. See fig. 2. At the bend in the stream I even sculpted in some rocks — the artist in me, I guess. Elsewhere I mounded up Sculptamold near the edge of the stream to give the ground some contour.

I completely filled the streambed with a thin coat of Sculptamold and "stepped" it in a couple places to allow for rapids later on. The primary object in all of this, however, is to completely cover up any holes that might allow our "water" to leak out. Give the Sculptamold a good two to three days to set up; all the moisture should be out of it within a week.

Cripple Creek Central RR
HO scale
curve radius = 24"
scale 1/2" = 1'-0"

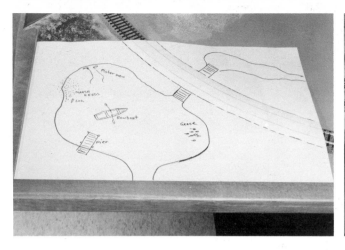

Fig. 1. Above: Draw a template of the lake and Cripple Creek on a sheet of paper; if you make a mistake, it's easy to start over. Tape down the template once you're happy with the shape and the size.

Above: Use a sharp utility knife to cut away the lake entirely and a chisel to scrape away the streambed — shallow at the point farthest from the lake and getting deeper as it approaches the culvert.

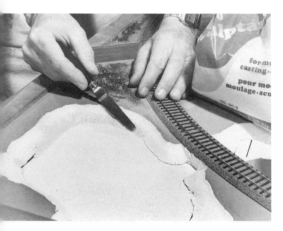

Fig. 2. After cutting the lake and stream banks to about a 45-degree angle, glue a piece of foam core in place to serve as the bed of the lake. When the cement has dried thoroughly, apply Sculptamold to the banks and the streambed. The object is to cover all seams and holes so the "water" doesn't leak out.

TINFOIL CULVERTS

To get our water from the stream, under the tracks, and into the lake, I fashioned a culvert. The first step was to cut two 1" x 1⁷⁄₁₆" rectangles of heavy-duty household foil. Then, one at a time, I carefully but tightly wrapped a piece of the foil around the threads of a ¼"-20 bolt, with approximately 1½" of threads (each half of the culvert is 1" long). See fig. 3. I twisted it tightly, with my fingers and thumbs pressing the foil into the threads.

Now, as you would with a nut, I unthreaded the foil. Then I poked a ballpoint pen into the end of the foil, opening it to a diameter of ½" to ⅝". This left an opening at the bottom that rests on the surface, giving the impression it continues underwater. Next, I glued the two ends of the culvert in place with carpenter's glue and, after they had dried, filled in around them with Sculptamold.

WATER AND EARTH

The white Sculptamold along the edges of the lake and stream looks like snow. Now it's time to turn this scene into summer.

First, I painted all surfaces, including the pond and stream bottoms, with the same flat tan latex paint we used for earlier projects. While it was still wet, I sprinkled on shades of green ground foam, darker greens near the water. Only natural, don't you think? Use a variety of textures and shades for a natural look. I also sprinkled fine sand along the lake banks and on the bottom of the streambed.

WATER FOR OUR PIKE

Since I won't *really* be putting water on the layout, I have to create the illusion of water. Using flat black latex paint, I painted the center of the lake. Not a big, black dot, mind you, but an

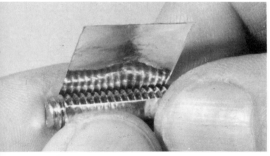
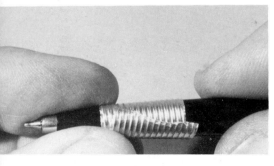
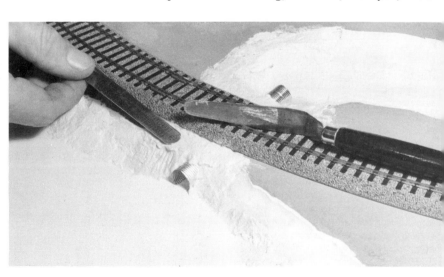

Fig. 3. Top left: To make a culvert, wrap a rectangle of heavy-duty aluminum foil around a bolt, overlapping it and pressing it into the grooves with your thumbs and fingers. **Left:** After unthreading the foil tube, slide it over the barrel of a ballpoint pen, then open it to about a ½" diameter. **Above:** After gluing each of the culvert halves in place, work some Sculptamold around them.

Products used

foam core, ¹/₄″ piece (slightly larger than lake)
ground foam (left over from previous construction)
latex paint, flat black (1 quart)
latex paint, flat tan (1 quart)
road gravel
satin gloss varnish
Sculptamold (3 pounds)
twine
yellow carpenter's glue

Tools used

chisel
palette knife
small paintbrush
small screwdriver
utility knife

Fig. 4. Small, smooth pebbles picked up in handfuls from along the shoulder of a road make good-looking river rocks (and they're cheap). The author placed them at the steps in the streambed to suggest rapids. Also, note the use of various textures and colors of ground foam, as well as the sheen the satin gloss gives to the stream. A nice effect without much effort or mess.

irregularly shaped area to suggest depth. I came within a inch or so of the edge of the pond where the tan suggests shallow water, feathering the black out to blend with the tan base.

While this was drying, I went out along the shoulder of a road and scooped up a handful of pebbles. I brought them home, washed them, and inspected them for cooties and other beasties. I picked out the smoothest stones and glued them in place at each of the Sculptamold "rapids." See fig. 4.

What we have now is a dry lake and streambed. Unless you're modeling California during the drought, what you want is the wet look. There are a couple ways of doing this; I chose the easier one. I poured a thin coat of satin gloss varnish (don't shake the can) in the stream, working from the shallow end toward the culvert. A small brush works well for coaxing the varnish into areas where it doesn't want to flow and into the culvert. When the stream looked good, I repeated the process in the lake.

WEEDS AND REEDS

I considered the project done until our resident detailer, Art Curren, stopped for a look at the layout. He made a suggestion that's really neat. He said that planting reeds along the banks of the lake would be easy.

Start by cutting and laying out 1″ strands of twine, as shown in fig. 5. Then, with a small screwdriver, poke a hole in the water near the shore. Drip a drop of white glue into the hole, lay the twine directly over the hole, and use the screwdriver to push the twine into the hole. It'll stand straight like cattails and other swampy growth. It's a neat idea that I've freely borrowed (with Art's permission). See the photo in fig. 5.

Now, when was the last time you saw trains that looked as spiffy as the ones on the CCC? Next month, veteran modeler Bob Hayden will change all that. ○

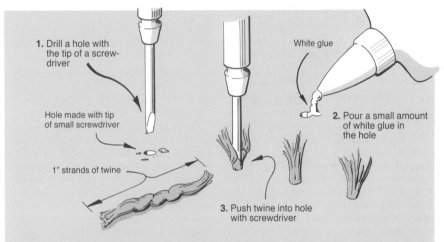

1. Drill a hole with the tip of a screwdriver

Hole made with tip of small screwdriver

1″ strands of twine

White glue

2. Pour a small amount of white glue in the hole

3. Push twine into hole with screwdriver

Fig. 5. The marsh grass around the fisherman's waders in the photo below is actually twine stuffed and glued into a hole. The author thought the idea was such a good one, he "borrowed" it from fellow Kalmbach employee and well-known modeler, Art Curren. While Art's idea wouldn't work well on plywood-base scenery, it's a natural on foam core.

Expert modeler Bob Hayden took two of our out-of-the-box HO cars and made them look like they'd been "rode hard and put away wet." They came out looking bad, and that's good: Shiny new freight cars are a rarity.

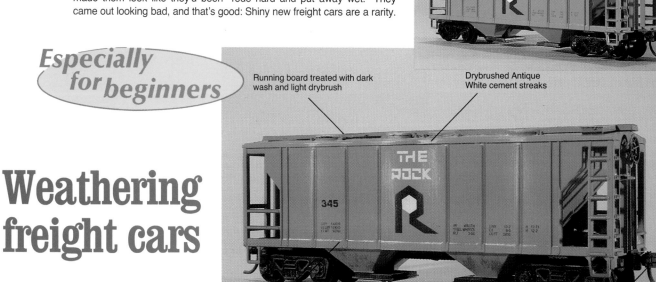

Weathering freight cars

It's a dirty job,
but you'll like the results

Running board treated with dark wash and light drybrush

Drybrushed Antique White cement streaks

Pastel chalk dust for cement powder

Drybrushed Rust on trucks, couplers, and underbody

A. L. Schmidt

BY BOB HAYDEN

WE MODEL RAILROADERS do a lot of things that real railroads can't or don't have to, and one of them is weather rolling stock. Railroad equipment operates out of doors, exposed to dirt, rain, wind, and sun, and after only a few trips the cars wear ample evidence of where they've been and what they've carried.

Passenger cars are washed from time to time, but freight cars just get dirtier and dirtier until it's time for a new coat of paint. In fact, clean and shiny cars are few and far between, so if you want your freight cars to look like the real thing, adding a coat of dirt and grime is every bit as important as the colors and lettering that come printed on the cars.

FINDING THE FIXIN'S

By far the most difficult step in weathering (and it's easy) is to gather the products you'll need. See fig. 1. There's nothing exotic, and a trip to your hobby shop will bag most of the items. Any art supply store will have the pastel chalk set and the brushes.

When you return from your quest, gather up the cars you want to weather and the spray can of Dullcote clear, flat coating and head outdoors (weather permitting). Whisk the cars with a soft brush to remove dust and lint, then give each three light applications of Dullcote, holding the spray can far

enough from the cars so the paint is almost dry when it hits the surface. Let the Dullcote dry for a couple of days — if you can stand the wait.

This clear, flat surface is important on two counts. First, it provides a protective coating impervious to our weathering treatments. This is a big confidence builder, because we'll be able to remove the weathering effects if we don't like them and then try again.

Second, the flat coating adds a microscopic rough finish to the car (artists call it "tooth"), which gives our weathering agents a good surface to stick to.

GRIME WASH AND WIPE

Generally it's best to weather light cars with dark colors and vice versa. We'll start by adding grime to the Mantua Santa Fe reefer in fig. 2. Mix 4 drops of Polly S Grimy Black with about a tablespoon of auto windshield washer fluid (the blue stuff) to make a dark-gray wash. Flow this onto the roof, ends, and sides of the car with a wide, soft brush.

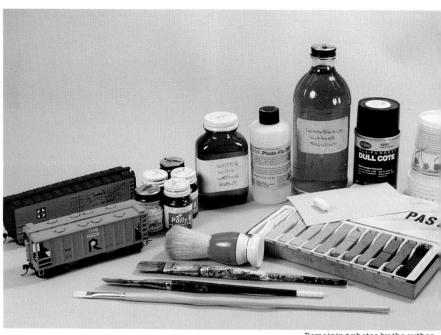

Remaining photos by the author

Thinned Grimy Black wash gives effect of dark dirt and grime

Drybrushed Rust on trucks and couplers

There's only one principle to follow, and it's easy to remember: Gravity lurks everywhere. As you apply the wash, make your brush strokes conform to the way gravity would make water flow. On a peaked roof that means from the center out to the sides, then down over the sides and ends.

Once you've applied the wash to all surfaces, start wiping it off with the brush. Keep stroking, bearing gravity in mind, until the surface of the car begins to dry and streak. Then put it aside to dry. The dark color will settle in recesses and around raised detail such as rivets, accentuating them. (Weathered cars look more detailed than their clean counterparts!) The thin coating of dark color over the orange paint makes the reefer look as if it has traveled hundreds of thousands of miles back and forth across America. Grubby, isn't it?

CHALK TREATMENTS

Let's weather the blue Model Die Casting Rock Island covered hopper with a light coating of light gray chalk, simulating dust from the cement it carries. Grind white and black pastel sticks to dust by rubbing them on coarse sandpaper, and save the dust in a paper cup.

Now brush the chalk onto the hopper car, remembering gravity just as before. Heap it on and brush it downward with a large, fluffy brush, as shown in fig. 3. Apply more than you think you need, because the next step will make most of it disappear.

Head back outdoors with the car and your can of Dullcote, and mist a light coat over the chalk powder. This will seal the chalk to the model so you can handle it without the powder coming off. Unfortunately, it will also make most of the powder invisible.

If you applied lots of chalk powder to the model, the Dullcote may render it just subtle enough to be pleasing, but if you're like me too much of the effect will disappear. See fig. 4. This means applying another coat of chalk, maybe two, and sealing again with Dullcote. The car in the photos took three applications of chalk and spray before I was satisfied with the effect, but that's the main strength of this technique: it's controllable.

Once you've got a couple of chalk weathering jobs under your belt, you can start experimenting with different colors of chalk dust. The easiest to use are earth tones, which represent dirt kicked up as the cars roll down the right-of-way. Don't overlook other colors, though, such as yellow to simulate grain dust on those big covered hoppers. Shades of brown are excellent for simulating rust peeking through failing paint.

Products used

Art materials
starter set of pastel chalk sticks (not oil pastels)
3/8" stiff-bristle bright brush
1/2" and 3/4" soft brushes

Paints
Polly S Antique White
Polly S Grimy Black
Polly S Rust
Testor's Dullcote

Miscellaneous
auto windshield-washer solvent
coarse sandpaper
paper cups
paper towels

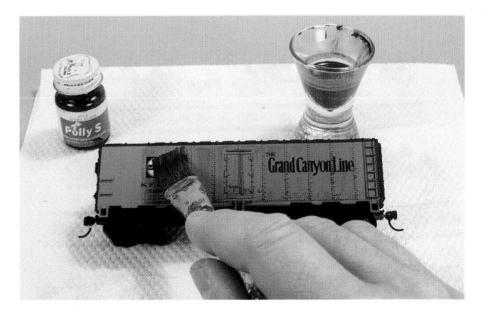

1. Left: These simple materials enough to weather a hundred ght cars in a hundred different ways.

Fig. 2. To weather this light-colored car, Bob flooded on a wash of greatly thinned Polly S Grimy Black. He wiped it off with a brush, using downward strokes to simulate the effects of grime, water, and gravity.

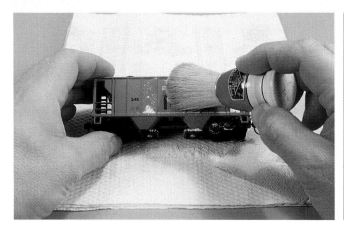

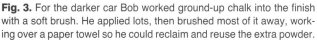

Fig. 3. For the darker car Bob worked ground-up chalk into the finish with a soft brush. He applied lots, then brushed most of it away, working over a paper towel so he could reclaim and reuse the extra powder.

Fig. 4. When you seal the chalk dust to the car by spraying it with Dullcote, most of the color disappears. No bother — just add more chalk and spray again until you build up the effect you like.

PAINTING WITH A DRY BRUSH

Our third weathering technique is called "drybrushing," and it's just as easy as the first two. The idea is to scrub the surface of the model with an almost-dry brush, so paint rubs off only on raised areas. This highlights the model's surface, adding color and revealing cast-in detail.

Use a stiff brush, such as an inexpensive China-bristle "bright" from the art store. Dip the bristles into Polly S Rust for about half their length, then brush out most of the paint onto a swatch of paper towel. (I used to brush the paint onto my left thumb until friends started talking behind my back.)

With most of the paint removed from the bristles it's now a dry brush, right? Scrub the brush across the truck sideframes as shown in fig. 5. If the brush is too dry, no color will stick to the model; if it's too wet, the paint will streak.

But if you've removed just the right amount of color on the paper towel, paint will adhere to only the raised details, accenting them. That's what we want. You can drybrush for quite a while on one load of paint, but after a sideframe or two it's time to go back to the well and start over.

Accents of Rust are appropriate anywhere on the underbody of the car, but don't overdo it. While you're working with the Rust, drybrush the couplers of each car. (Couplers, being critical to safety, must be examined for cracks and flaws. They can't be painted, so they rust.)

After Rust, the best color for drybrushing is off-white. Use Polly S Antique White to add heavy cement stains to the sides of the hopper beneath each roof hatch and around the hatch on the roof. Again, don't overdo it.

A LITTLE RUNNING BOARD COMBO

Let's finish with a bit of weathering trickery. The molded running board on the MDC covered hopper is five or six times heavier than the lacy punched-metal grating on the real thing, but we can improve its appearance by combining two of the techniques we've learned.

Reach for the Grimy Black wash we used on the orange reefer and flow an ample coat over the running board, be-

ing careful to fill all the tiny rectangular recesses, meanwhile keeping the color off the sides of the molding. Let the wash dry; as it does the color will settle into the holes and create a see-through look.

About a half-hour after applying the dark wash, lightly drybrush the raised surface of the running board with Polly S Antique White. Be careful to keep the white out of the depressions. The effect is right when the raised grating pattern stands out against the dark background. The running board looks a lot better simply because we've simulated light and shadow with white and black paints. See fig. 6.

Armed with three easy weathering techniques, you're now ready to filth-up all your freight cars — except one. Choose one car that looks particularly good and leave it alone. (Okay, hit the trucks and couplers with a little drybrushed Rust.) Having one pristine car in the fleet will provide a strong counterpoint to your majority of grubbies.

What's next? Well, next month Jim Kelly will add something to our HO scale layout that's already there — a vacant lot. See you then. ✿

Fig. 5. Above: You can indeed paint with a dry brush! After working the brush on a paper towel to remove all but a residue of paint, stroke it across the trucks and underbody.
Fig. 6. Right: Some simple trickery vastly improves the look of the running board on the MDC covered hopper. The depressions were darkened with a black wash, while the raised areas were highlighted by drybrushing white.

Building a building that isn't there

Plus putting together that first polyester kit

BY JIM KELLY

THIS MONTH we're presenting the old demolished building trick, a nifty ploy that adds interest to Main St. and gives us three buildings for the price of two. (It's just that one has been torn down and only the basement remains.)

TWO KITS, TWO MATERIALS

First we put together our two store buildings. Both were easy kits, but one was a little easier than the other because of the materials used. The red brick structure is a plastic kit in Walthers' Cornerstone series; the yellow one is by Magnuson and consists of castings made in polyester resin.

This is the first kit we've encountered in this beginners series that uses casting resin, and you'll discover it requires more patience than plastic. First of all, our handy-dandy liquid plastic cement won't bond this material. You need to use either a CA (cyanoacrylate adhesive, also called super glue) or a two-part epoxy. The instructions with the kit cover using these adhesives very well, so make sure you read them. I assembled my kit with a gap-filling CA.

The second difficulty with polyester structures is that the walls often are not as square or as flat as we might like. These parts are made by pouring the resin into rubber molds, and they just don't have the same precision as parts made by injecting molten plastic into steel molds.

Also, a harsh chemical reaction takes place between the resin and the rubber. To extend mold life the manufacturer pulls the castings as soon as possible. As a result, some of the parts may not be entirely cured and can be slightly distorted in the process.

A. L. Schmidt

This month we add a drugstore and pool hall to Main St. Sandwiched between them is the hole that's all that remains of Earl's Barber Shop. Our two building kits differ in an important way. The red one is plastic; the yellow one is polyester and requires different adhesives.

Why, you may ask, does a manufacturer use a process with such inherent problems? The answer lies in economics. You can make a lot of rubber molds for a few hundred dollars, whereas $25,000 won't go far when it comes to buying tooling for an injection-molded kit.

Full size for HO scale

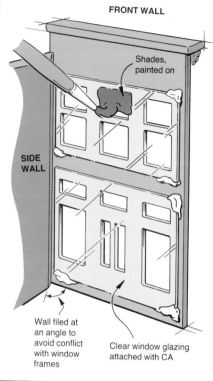

FRONT WALL

SIDE WALL

Shades, painted on

Wall filed at an angle to avoid conflict with window frames

Clear window glazing attached with CA

FIG. 1. WORKING WITH POLYESTER

Upper left: The front wall of our yellow building was considerably bowed. To correct this we first sanded the back flat on medium-grade emery paper, working on a flat surface. **Above left:** The sidewalls bowed in toward each other. We straightened them by adding a center brace between our styrene roof supports. **Above:** The thick sidewalls would have interfered with the front windows and needed surgery.

FIG. 2. ADDING THE BUILDING BASE

Left: We came in with our HO bulldozer to level the building site. **Below left:** We cemented on a base made from 3/16″ foam core board. **Below:** The sidewalk and curb were made using ever-handy Evergreen styrene.

PAINTING THE MODELS

We painted the walls for both kits before assembling them. First came the old mortar trick. We painted the red walls with Polly S Concrete straight from the bottle, then lightly wiped the paint off the brick surfaces with paper towels, leaving it in the mortar lines. If you try this, make sure to use Polly S or another acrylic-based paint. Lacquer-based paints (such as Floquil) will attack the plastic and spoil the kit.

Next we painted the details. Let the photos be your color guide. It's amazing how good those walls began to look at this stage. For the windows we cemented swatches of clear plastic (included in the kit) behind them, then painted on shades, using Polly S Mud.

Finally came the fun part, putting the walls together. It's important to test-fit the parts carefully. Use a small flat file (8″ shall we say) to achieve good fits.

As shown in fig. 1, the front wall on the polyester building had a pronounced bow towards the top. I flattened the back by rubbing it against a sheet of medium-grade emery paper laid on a flat, hard surface. Incidentally, this bow isn't noticed on the finished building. These structures have a way of looking just fine once you get them assembled. In fact, they're a bit better off for their imperfections. Real buildings settle and twist with age and aren't perfect either.

A HOLE IN THE GROUND

Figure 2 shows how we installed the buildings on the layout. First we used a scraper to remove the Sculptamold we'd used earlier to form a shoulder on the road. Passersby said the resultant rubble was neat, so we saved some of it to use later. We made a base for our new buildings from 3/16″ foam core board, available at art supply stores.

BASE CONSTRUCTION

Evergreen sidewalk material (1/2″ square)

Curb, styrene strip, edge rounded

Parking area is feathered to road surface with Sculptamold, painted Grimy Black

Shims, see text

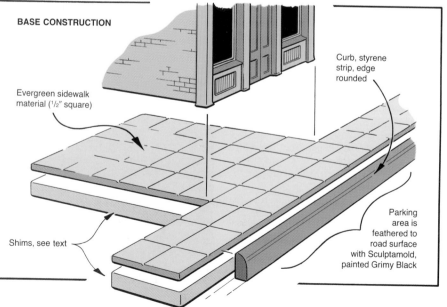

FIG. 3. MODELING EARL'S BARBER SHOP

Below: We suggested what's left of Earl's by making a cardstock template, masking off the adjoining walls, and then painting that shape. Look at the color photos, and you'll quickly get the idea.
Right: Cutting a hole in our foam core tabletop was very easy.

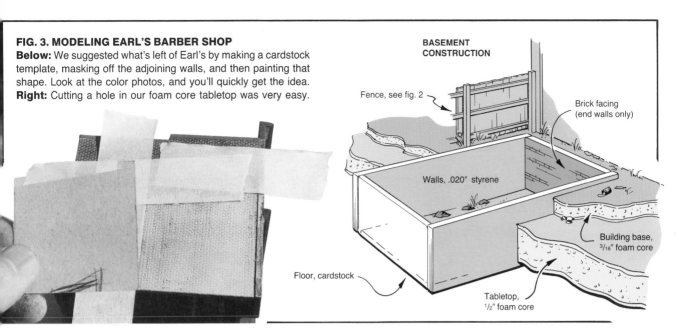

BASEMENT CONSTRUCTION

Fence, see fig. 2

Brick facing (end walls only)

Walls, .020″ styrene

Building base, 3/16″ foam core

Floor, cardstock

Tabletop, 1/2″ foam core

Next came the sidewalk, cut from Evergreen's styrene sidewalk material. We cut bases for the buildings from the same material to get them shimmed to the same height. The sidewalk still didn't look high enough, so we shimmed it and the building bases up some more with strips of .060″ sheet styrene. The curb is .060″ x .100″ styrene strip.

Products used

Evergreen styrene
155 .060″ x .100″ strips (1 pkg.)
4518 scribed sidewalk (1 pkg.)
9060 .060″ sheet (1 pkg.)

Magnuson Models
537 "Practice kit" store

Northeastern
3004 HO 1 x 6s (1 pkg.)
3012 HO 2 x 4s (1 pkg.)
3040 HO 6 x 6s (1 pkg.)

Pacer
435 Zap-a-Gap adhesive

Polly S paint
500014 Grimy Black
500030 Blue
500051 Grass Green
500082 Concrete
500305 Battleship Gray
500308 Brown
500820 Earth

Preiser
0027 workers
0031 figures with benches

Railway Models
SS0401 plastic brick sheet

Testor
3502 liquid plastic cement

Wm. K. Walthers
3000 Don's Shoe Store

If you've never worked with sheet styrene, you'll find it a wonder. All you have to do is scribe a line with a hobby knife, snap the plastic, and it'll break cleanly just where you want it to. We painted these parts with Polly S Concrete.

Since the layout surface is 1/2″ foam core board, it was easy to cut into it with a hobby knife and dig out a hole for our basement. Our hole is 2″ x 3 1/4″. Let's say it once lay under Earl's Barber Shop. Earl never learned to do anything but crew cuts and paid no attention to the termites eating up his mostly empty establishment.

It just so happened that our hole fell over one of the splice plates on the underside of the railroad, so it was easy to excavate down to the top of that plate, then glue in a basement floor cut from the cardboard provided as roof material for the pool hall.

WALLS, A FENCE, AND LOTS OF JUNK

We scored and snapped the basement walls from the .060″ styrene. The two end ones were faced with plastic sheet material for a little variety. After painting the walls and floor Concrete, we tossed in a little gravel, foam grass, and some junk. Included in this last category were pipes and steps left over from the playground set used in the June issue, some of the rubble mentioned above, and a few dozen short lengths of stripwood. All of this was bonded by soaking it with dilute yellow glue applied with an eyedropper.

We worked the building base into the existing scenery with Sculptamold, a scenery product available from hobby and craft stores. Once this material had dried, we painted on some of our flat tan latex paint and sprinkled on several grades and colors of ground foam. A little more dilute yellow glue helped hold all of this in place.

Figure 3 shows how we painted the sides of the two buildings to make it look as if Earl's Barber Shop had once butted against them. Some of the signs we added are left over from the Tyco drugstore kit used for our June project.

Even Earl is smart enough to avoid lawsuits, so we made a stripwood fence to put in front of the hole, as shown in fig. 4. Single-edge razor blades work great for simple wood projects like this, or you can use a hobby knife.

Well, that about covers it. Tune in next month when we get out of town and start constructing hills on the back side of the backdrop. A little carefree scenery building should be good for the soul after the careful work required for building structures. ⚐

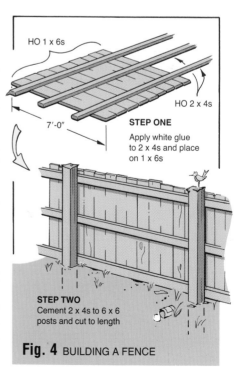

HO 1 x 6s

HO 2 x 4s

7′-0″

STEP ONE
Apply white glue to 2 x 4s and place on 1 x 6s

STEP TWO
Cement 2 x 4s to 6 x 6 posts and cut to length

Fig. 4 BUILDING A FENCE

Popcorn scenery

Using a common packing
material to add a hill
to our beginners layout

BY JEFF WILSON

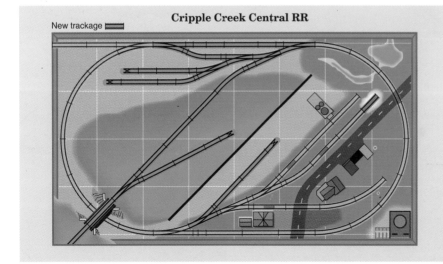

UNTIL NOW, the half of our HO scale Cripple Creek Central layout away from the city has been rather barren. As you can see in the photos, that has changed dramatically. Scenic details such as hills, bridges, and grades add a great deal of interest to any layout, so that's just what we decided to add this month. If you've never attempted scenery before, don't be afraid to try: The methods we're using are easy and quick, aren't messy, and produce very good results.

TRACKWORK

Our first step is to complete the trackwork (the new track is highlighted on the track plan). The main addition is a branch that goes up a grade, crosses our main line, and heads off the edge of the layout. This line can be used for a future extension, but for now it will just simulate a branch line and give our railroad another connection (along with the interchange track) with the outside world. To give trains a reason to use the line, we included a siding that will be the site of a future industry.

We've also added a runaround track and two storage tracks at the foot of the hill, and another spur on the city side of the layout. It's important that all track leading to the grade be in place prior to adding the hill. The switches and track for the storage tracks and industrial spur may be added later if you wish.

Note that a terminal section is the last piece of track on the grade. This is necessary because of the power-routing feature of the Kato switches. Wiring this section provides power to the siding on the hill when the turnout is thrown for it. More on this later.

ADDING A GRADE

Begin by using a large putty knife to scrape away the ground foam in the area of the new trackwork. Fit the new track sections into place, as always making sure that the track is in proper alignment and the rail joints are secure. Lay a sheet of 3/16" foam core under the track that is to be elevated. This will serve as the roadbed.

The grade should begin 6" past the turnout leading to the branch. Be sure all track joints are secure and the track lines up properly. Using a pencil, trace a line about 1" outside the edge of the Unitrack onto the foam core. Remove the foam core and use a utility knife to cut along the outline. Using the knife again, bevel the bottom edge of the foam core where the elevation begins. The grade must begin smoothly, so there are no kinks in any rail joints.

Place the roadbed under the track as

Cripple Creek Central RR

New trackage

this really is our HO scale Cripple Creek
al layout! The back side hadn't received
much attention, so we decided to add a
h line on a hill. Photo by A. L. Schmidt.

shown in fig. 1, again making sure everything lines up properly. Trace the
outline of the roadbed onto the layout
board, then remove both the roadbed
and the track that will be upon it.

BRIDGE AND RISERS

To determine the height of the bridge,
I measured our tallest piece of equipment and added $3/16''$ for clearance. The
bottom of the bridge is $2\frac{3}{4}''$ above the
layout board and $2\frac{3}{8}''$ above the rails of
the track below. Our Atlas switcher has
had no problems pulling two and three
cars up the resulting grade. If you have
taller equipment and want to make your
bridge higher, test your locomotive to
make sure it will make it up the hill.

Cut the risers from a $3''$-wide strip of
foam core. Riser placement, height,
and construction are shown in fig. 2.
The size of the riser braces isn't vital;
just be sure they're square where they
meet the riser and layout board.

Glue the risers in place with yellow
glue, using the guidelines you previ-
ously traced on the layout board. Place
the two risers that serve as bridge abutments $8\frac{5}{8}''$ part (for an Atlas plate
girder bridge). If you use a different
bridge, place the abutments so each of
their faces is set in about $3/16''$ from the
ends of the bridge. The abutment inside
the curve is placed $6\frac{1}{4}''$ from the center
of the lower track. This provides room to
add a road and other details later.

Place the roadbed on the risers. Don't
worry about the bridge yet — we'll cut
a gap in the roadbed for it later. Sight
along the roadbed, making sure the
grade is smooth. If it isn't, adjust the
height of the intermediate risers by
trimming them or adding cardstock
shims. Once it's straight, use yellow
glue to secure the roadbed to the risers,
placing weights on top of the roadbed to
hold everything in place. When this
has dried, cut and install additional
risers to fit between those that are already in place. We tried to make sure
we had a riser about every $4''$.

Cut out the roadbed between the
bridge abutments. Cut notches above
the abutments so the bridge drops into
place as in fig. 3. Taper the roadbed near
the abutments to match the width of the
bridge. Glue the bridge in place with
Walthers Goo. We'll lay the Unitrack directly through the bridge, simulating a
ballasted deck bridge. Add wings to the
abutments using $1''$-wide strips of foam
core. Bevel the inside edges of these with

FIG. 1. ROADBED
Be sure the track lines up properly before marking the location of the roadbed on the layout.

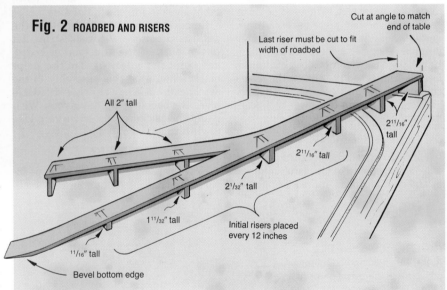

Fig. 2 ROADBED AND RISERS

Cut at angle to match end of table

Last riser must be cut to fit width of roadbed

All 2" tall

$2^{11}/_{16}''$ tall

$2^{11}/_{16}''$ tall

$2^{1}/_{32}''$ tall

$1^{11}/_{32}''$ tall

Initial risers placed every 12 inches

$^{11}/_{16}''$ tall

Bevel bottom edge

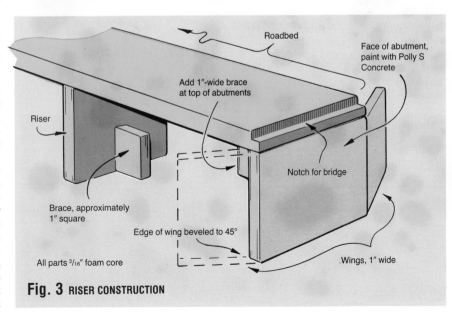

Roadbed

Face of abutment, paint with Polly S Concrete

Add 1"-wide brace at top of abutments

Riser

Notch for bridge

Brace, approximately 1" square

Edge of wing beveled to 45°

All parts $3/16''$ foam core

Wings, 1" wide

Fig. 3 RISER CONSTRUCTION

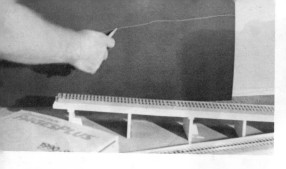

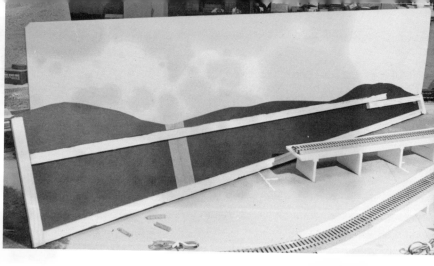

FIG. 4. BACKDROP

Above: Trace the outline of a hill onto the illustration board, then cut along the line.
Right: Use wood strips to set the hill away from the sky backdrop, then glue in place. Use packing tape to splice the illustration board.

the utility knife, paint them Polly S Concrete, and glue them into place.

Replace the track. Use an awl or hobby knife to poke holes in the roadbed and layout board for the wires from the switch and terminal track, and thread these wires into place. Secure the track with Goo. We used a razor saw to cut the last piece of track at an angle where it meets the table. Our bumper is simply a piece of clear plastic cut from the cover of a box of Preiser figures (similar to the one on the interchange track) and secured with Goo. This can be seen in the lower right corner of the lead photo.

BACKDROP

We constructed the backdrop on this side of the layout in the same manner as the city backdrop, but we decided to

create our own scene instead of using a commercial one. Start by positioning a piece of illustration board in front of the sky backdrop. Use a light-colored pencil to trace the outline of a hill, keeping in mind that the terrain we're adding will contact the backdrop above table level as you see in fig. 4.

Remove the board and cut along the outline. Glue 1/2" x 3/4" wood strips flat to the back of the illustration board, and paint the outer edges of the strips black. Then glue this assembly to the sky backdrop. When this has dried, replace the backdrop on the layout. We'll paint the backdrop after we've added the hill to the layout.

SCENERY

Now the real fun starts. The steps involved in creating scenery are shown in

fig. 5. Associate editor Jim Kelly chose Styrofoam popcorn as the scenery base. This common packing material is lightweight, makes a good base for scenery material, and is ideal for forming rolling hills, which is the effect we wanted.

Begin by spreading the popcorn around the elevated track, to the bridge and backdrop. Then add popcorn and shape your hill until you've achieved the effect that you're looking for. For the scenic base we decided to use Rigid-Wrap, which is a plaster-impregnated gauze similar to that used by doctors for making casts. This material is easy and very neat to use. If you have trouble finding it, contact Activa Products, P. O. Box 472, Westford, MA 01886; telephone 508-692-9300.

It took us about three rolls to complete our hill. Cut the gauze into sections

FIG. 5. BUILDING THE HILL

Right: Begin by spreading some popcorn into the shape of the hill.
Below left: Then apply the Rigid-Wrap over the popcorn, making sure to overlap the pieces slightly.
Below middle: Once the Rigid-Wrap has dried, start applying the Sculptamold with a putty knife.
Below right: Use a wet paintbrush to smooth the Sculptamold and to add some scenic effects.

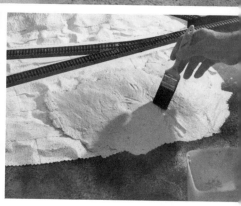

about 6″ long. Briefly soak each strip in water and then apply it over the popcorn. Don't worry if you get some plaster on the backdrop — we'll take care of that later. Overlap the pieces slightly, using smaller sections to shape tight spaces such as the area around the bridge abutments.

Once the Rigid-Wrap has dried, add Sculptamold to the entire hill. Use a putty knife to apply it, working it over the base to a thickness of about ⅛″. Apply the Sculptamold right up to the backdrop, then slide a putty knife along the backdrop to keep the Sculptamold from attaching itself. Work in small batches.

After applying the Sculptamold to a section of the hill, use a paintbrush soaked in water to smooth the surface. You can use the brush and knife to create scenic effects. For example, to make a rivulet, use the brush to make an indentation running down a hill. You can also create more elaborate rock formations, as Jim did in fig. 6 at the base of the bridge. Once the Sculptamold has set, the rest of the scenery procedure is the same as it is for flat territory (fig. 7).

Products used

Activa
999 Rigid-Wrap (3 rolls)

Amaco
Sculptamold (3-pound bag)

Atlas
85 plate girder bridge

Kato Unitrack
2120 4½″ straight (5)
2150 9¾″ straight (9)
2220 curve (1)
2850 left-hand turnout (1)
2851 right-hand turnout (4)
5101 bumper (4)

Polly S paint
410070 Roof Brown
410082 Concrete
500051 Grass Green

Woodland Scenics
44 turf, burnt grass
49 blended turf, mixed
62 coarse turf, burnt
63 coarse turf, light green
65 coarse turf, dark green

Miscellaneous
colored pencil (white or yellow)
flat tan latex paint
paintbrushes, various sizes
putty knife
Walthers Goo
yellow carpenter's glue
1/16″ illustration board, 22″ x 28″
3/16″ foam core, 12″ x 66″
½″ x ¾″ x 8'-0″ wood strips (2)

FINAL DETAILS

Use a damp sponge to clean any stray drops of plaster or Sculptamold from the Unitrack, layout table, and backdrop. Paint the illustration board with your tan paint. When that has dried, paint over it with Polly S Grass Green. Spread the paint with a small, flat brush, working the paint horizontally until it's almost dry. This lets some of the tan show through, helping to blend the backdrop with the scenery. If the effect isn't what you're looking for, don't be afraid to slap some more tan on the backdrop and start over.

While this is drying, you can remove the popcorn from under the hill where the backdrop had held it in place. Some of it probably came tumbling out when you removed the backdrop. Don't worry about taking it out — the hill will stand by itself with no problem.

Connect the wires from the terminal track to the power pack (along with the wires to the original terminal section), making sure the polarity is the same on both. Clean your track with a Bright Boy, and your trains are once again ready to go!

Next month we'll be back to wire all of those new switches we added. And, since it's now rather difficult to see through the backdrop to operate your trains, we'll also show you how to add the handheld throttle you see in the photo at the top of page 42. ⌀

FIG. 6. SPECIAL EFFECTS
Below: Special effects, such as this rockwork, are easy to do. Use a brush and putty knife to form the Sculptamold while it is still wet, and apply the scenery as in fig. 7. Use a 1″ flat brush to stain the rockwork with a 1:1 mix of Polly S Roof Brown and water. Apply the wash beginning at the top so it can flow into crevices. If the wash is too dark, dip your brush into plain water and repeat the process. Once this is dry, apply coarse foam to the base of the formation and fix it with diluted glue spray.

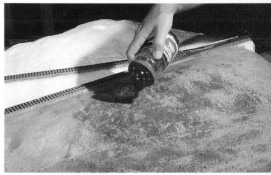

FIG. 7. APPLYING THE SCENERY
Top: After carefully removing the backdrop, go ahead and paint the hill with the same flat latex paint that we used on the layout board.
Middle: While the paint is still wet, apply various colors of ground foam. We used both blended green and burnt grass turf for the base, allowing some of the ground color to show through for realism. After doing that we added dark as well as light green coarse turf.
Bottom: Once the ground foam was applied, spray it with a 3:1 mix of water and yellow glue.

Walkaround control for a small layout

Featuring a control panel with raised track lines

Chris Becker

Our throttle has an eight-foot tether that allows us to run trains from anywhere around the layout and watch the action up close. We made raised lines on the control panel with styrene strips

BY JIM KELLY

YOU'VE ALL heard the story about the fellow who painted himself into the corner. Well, that's just what we did to ourselves on the HO scale Cripple Creek Central when we added the backdrop down the middle, described in our July issue. The problem didn't become evident, though, until last month, when we added switches and spur tracks on the far side of the backdrop and discovered we couldn't see them from our power pack position on the right front corner.

One solution would be to move the power pack toward the middle of the layout, which we could do by adding a small shelf under the front edge. With all the new switching possibilities, though, we decided we'd really like a handheld throttle. With this we could move close to the action and enjoy our switching that much more.

Also, we decided to build a control panel with push buttons for throwing the turnouts. It was considerable work, so if you'd prefer you can continue with Kato's blue control boxes.

HANDHELD THROTTLE

Our new throttle is a Voltroller from Scale Shops. Such a specialized item can be hard to find in hobby shops, but if necessary you can order direct. The address is 111 E. Adler, Stockton, CA 95204-4449. Our assembled throttle cost $49.98.

If you want to assemble the throttle yourself, you can buy a kit for $29.95. This would require soldering electronics components to a printed-circuit board. It shouldn't be too difficult, and if you're looking for a good first electronics assembly project, this could be it.

The power source for our Voltroller is the Bachmann power pack we've used until now. We hid it under the hill, as shown in fig. 1. Getting at it is easy — just lift the corner of the backdrop.

To cover the holes in the train board left by moving the throttle, simply glue some cardboard over them, paint them with flat tan latex paint, and sprinkle on some ground foam scenery material. You can bond it with dilute white glue applied with an eyedropper.

To install the throttle you first need to install the socket in the edge of the layout. I was able to carve a hole in the wood edge with a hobby knife, working carefully and checking with the socket as I went along. Next I soldered the wires to . . . .

SOLDERING WIRES

Traitor! Turncoat! Even worse, I can hear some of you screaming. This series wasn't supposed to have any hard stuff like soldering!

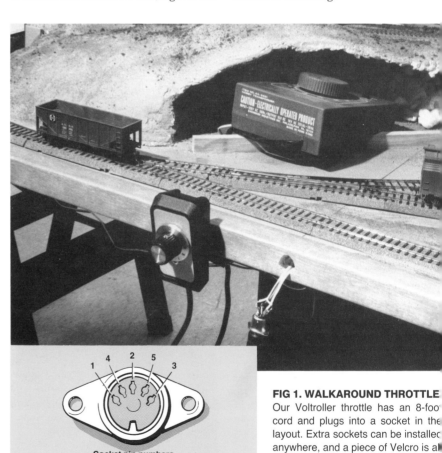

Socket pin numbers

FIG 1. WALKAROUND THROTTLE
Our Voltroller throttle has an 8-foot cord and plugs into a socket in the layout. Extra sockets can be installed anywhere, and a piece of Velcro is all that's needed to hang the throttle

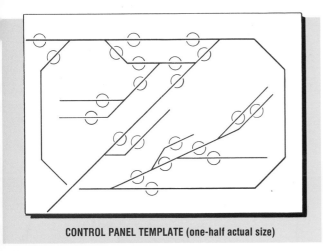

CONTROL PANEL TEMPLATE (one-half actual size)

FIG. 2. MAKING THE CONTROL PANEL
Above left: We made a paper template and taped it to .060″ plastic.
Above right: A light tap on the awl marked push-button center holes.
Below left: To represent the individual track lines, we carefully

cemented on plastic strips, using a brush to flow in the liquid cement.
Below right: We spray-painted the panel, let the paint dry thoroughly, and sanded off the surfaces of the track lines by rubbing the face of the panel against emery paper taped to a flat surface. It took patience.

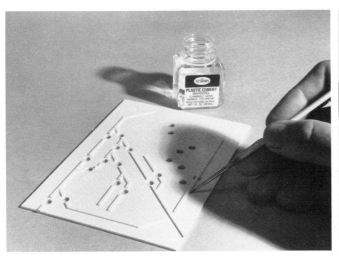

Well, sorry, but soldering, at least soldering electrical wires, isn't all that tough, and it's something you'll want to learn sooner or later if you go much farther in model railroading.

First you need decent tools and materials. The little Radio Shack iron I used works great and cost less than $6. The directions on the back of the package are excellent.

The first thing we're going to do is solder the wires to the socket. Step one is tinning the wires and the socket prongs. Tinning means coating the surface with a thin layer of solder, and it makes soldering so much easier that you should learn to do it automatically on any soldering job.

Using a pair of wire strippers, strip about ½″ of insulation from the end of a wire and dab a little flux on it with a toothpick. Even though the rosin-core solder we're using has flux in it, I like to add some paste flux, as it makes the job go that much easier. The flux heats to a boil almost instantaneously, cleaning the surfaces and helping the solder flow rapidly.

Since we're soldering electrical wires, make sure you use a rosin flux and not an acid one. Acid flux causes electrical connections to corrode.

Lay the wire end on the tip of your iron, and touch the wire with solder from above. The electronics solder we're using is quite thin and will melt and flow into the wire almost magically. Presto! You have tinned the wire. Practice on several more wires, and then tin the pins on the socket, remembering to apply flux first.

We need three or more hands for many soldering projects, but the way to get by with only two is to anchor the object you're soldering to, in this case the socket. I just fastened mine to a piece of plywood with masking tape.

One problem I quickly discovered is that the numbers on the socket pins are extremely difficult to see, even under a magnifier, and their order defies logic. Figure 1 also shows the pin numbering. Follow the directions as to which wire goes where.

Add a little flux to the tinned wire, hold it against the pin, and apply the

iron so it touches both. Within a couple of seconds the two should be joined.

THE BIG SECRET

There's one simple secret to good soldering — plenty of heat. And make sure you're heating the work so that it melts the solder, rather than just dripping melted solder onto the joint. This latter can result in a "cold" joint, where a solid bond has not really been made. Good solder joints look shiny.

In soldering wires, if the bond isn't made within three seconds something's wrong. These are the possibilities:

● The soldering iron has not been plugged in long enough.

● The tip of the iron isn't clean and won't transfer heat properly. Wipe it with a sponge dampened with water and make sure it's tinned.

● The tip has become pitted or misshapen. File it to a proper shape or replace it.

● The threads of the tip have become corroded or loose and aren't making good electrical contact within the socket. High heat encourages both of these

FIG. 3. INSTALLING THE CONTROL PANEL

Top left: We used the control panel to mark the location and cut a hole in the hillside with a razor saw. **Middle left:** We cut a strip of black cardboard 6″ high, then scored and folded corners to make a box the panel would fit in. After marking where the scenery intersected with the box, we cut it to fit. **Bottom left:** Wood strips measuring ¼″ square are glued in the box to support the panel.

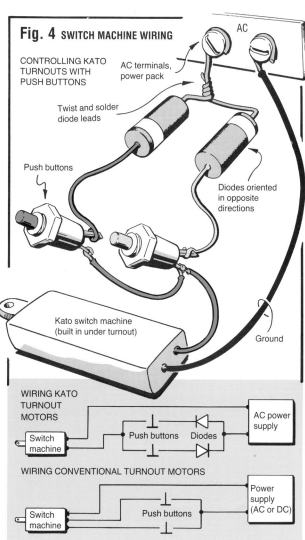

Fig. 4 SWITCH MACHINE WIRING

CONTROLLING KATO TURNOUTS WITH PUSH BUTTONS

AC terminals, power pack

Twist and solder diode leads

Push buttons

Diodes oriented in opposite directions

Kato switch machine (built in under turnout)

Ground

WIRING KATO TURNOUT MOTORS

Switch machine — Push buttons — Diodes — AC power supply

WIRING CONVENTIONAL TURNOUT MOTORS

Switch machine — Push buttons — Power supply (AC or DC)

---

conditions. Usually just screwing the tip out and in again will solve the problem. If not, clean the threads with a small wire brush.

- The work isn't clean. Shine it with emery cloth or sandpaper, and remember to use the flux.

Having soldered foot-long wires to the socket pins, I was ready to install the socket. Using a hobby knife I carefully carved a hole in the layout's wood trim, checking carefully with the socket as I progressed. Then I connected the wires under the layout, soldering the joints and wrapping them with 3″ lengths of electrician's tape.

THE CONTROL PANEL

The idea of recessing the control panel into the hillside seemed radical, but everyone I've asked likes it, and I like it too.

Step 1 is making the control panel itself, using .060″ sheet styrene. You'll find that a template for it is included in fig. 2. Make a 200 percent enlargement of that template — this is done most easily on a copy machine. Using a scriber, awl, or even a nail, you'll find you can transfer center marks for the push-button holes and the track lines to the plastic without cutting through the paper.

Next, cut the holes for the push buttons. I twirled in the first couple with a hobby knife, double-checking with a button as I went along. Once I'd proven to myself it could be done with just a hobby knife, I cheated and finished the job on a drill press.

Then I added the track lines using styrene strips, making sure that I left enough space for the push-button nuts. I painted the panel with a spray can and let it dry most of the day. Next, I carefully sanded off the paint to leave raised white lines.

Control panel installation is shown in fig. 3. I cut a hole in the scenery, then fitted it with a black cardboard liner. I touched up the scenery around the recess by filling the gaps with Sculptamold, the scenery material we've used throughout this project. Once it had dried I painted it with our tan latex and sprinkled on ground foam.

WIRING THE PANEL

The Kato turnout motors are different from others I've seen in that they

48

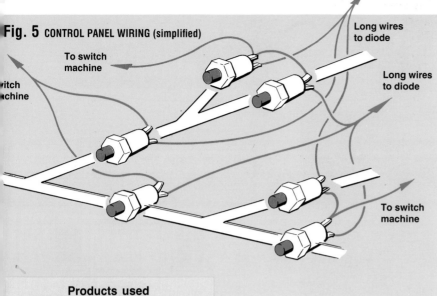

Fig. 5 CONTROL PANEL WIRING (simplified)

To switch machine

Long wires to diode

Long wires to diode

switch machine

To switch machine

Products used

Evergreen Scale Models
134 .030" x .080" styrene strips
9060 .060" styrene sheet

Kadee
321 uncoupling magnets (3 pkgs.)

Radio Shack
64-004 rosin-core solder
64-021 rosin soldering paste flux
64-2066A 30-watt soldering gun
64-2348 electrical tape
275-1571A subminiature, momentary-contact push buttons (11 pkgs.)
276-1114 2.5A, 1,000PIV silicon diodes
278-1224 hookup wire (2 pkgs.)

Scale Shops
Voltroller walkaround throttle

Testor
Model Master 1913 medium green spray paint

Miscellaneous
strippers, electric wire
1/16" x 30" x 40" mounting board, black

have only two wires to hook up. I don't want to get bogged down in how they work — suffice it to say the turnout is thrown by reversing the polarity of the current the machines receive. A polarized power source is required, and this we created by attaching a pair of diodes to the AC terminals on our Bachmann power pack, as shown in fig. 4.

All you need to know about the diodes is that they conduct current in only one direction. Alternating current, AC, reverses its polarity 60 times a second, but our diodes eliminate the reverse-polarity waves on each side of the circuit.

To throw the turnouts we're using subminiature, momentary-contact push buttons from Radio Shack. I chose these because Radio Shack has stores all over the country. One problem, though, at least in the Milwaukee area, is that they stock these buttons only four packages

deep (each package has two buttons).

You can do as I did and go to three different stores, you can ask them to order the buttons for you, or you can get similar buttons at a different electronics store that stocks in more depth. Just make sure they have the momentary-contact feature, or you'll burn out your switch machines.

Figure 5 shows how the control panel was wired. This is a simple job, but time-consuming. (It took me 6 hours.) Here's a check list for doing it:

☐ To each black push button solder one long (8") and one short (3") green wire.

☐ To each red push button solder one long and one short red wire.

☐ Install push buttons in panel, a red and black pair for each turnout, using lock washers behind panel.

☐ For each button pair, twist and solder the short wires together.

☐ Combine all long red wires, five wires in one group and six in the other. Connect to a single wire running to one of the diodes and solder.

☐ Follow the same procedure with the long green wires.

☐ Join all the black wires from the turnout machines and connect to the ground terminal on the power pack.

☐ Run a red wire from each short wire pair to red wire on switch machine.

☐ If button doesn't throw the turnout direction you want, reverse connections to switch machine wires.

☐ Make sure all connections are soldered and taped.

Now sit back and enjoy your nifty control panel and a little walkaround operation. We've added more Kadee magnetic uncoupling ramps to the railroad and have been having a great time switching cars. And we hope you'll be here next month when Sam Swanson shows us how to build that first scratchbuilt structure. ☼

Full size for HO scale

VAN

This humble abode sits on the highest hill on our "Especially for beginners" HO scale layout.

Fig. 1 TEMPLATES (Full size for HO scale)

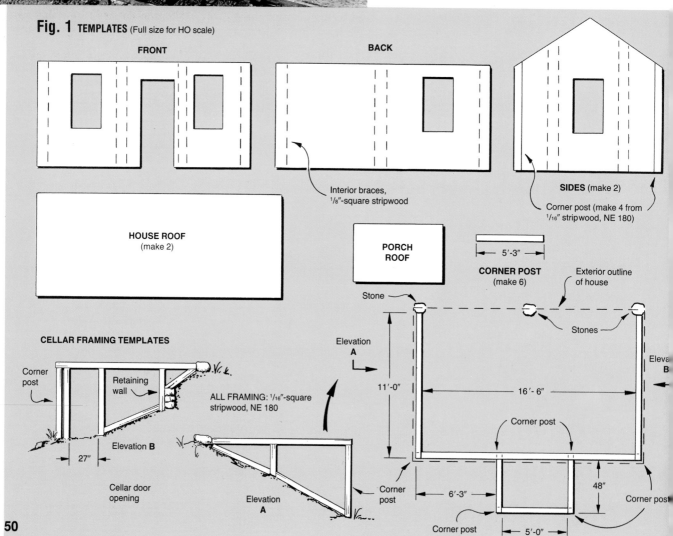

FRONT

BACK

Interior braces, 1/8"-square stripwood

SIDES (make 2)

Corner post (make 4 from 1/16" stripwood, NE 180)

HOUSE ROOF
(make 2)

PORCH ROOF

5'-3"

CORNER POST
(make 6)

Exterior outline of house

Stone

Stones

CELLAR FRAMING TEMPLATES

Corner post

Retaining wall

ALL FRAMING: 1/16"-square stripwood, NE 180

Elevation A

Elevation B

11'-0"

16'-6"

Corner post

27"

Elevation B

Cellar door opening

Elevation A

Corner post

6'-3"

48"

Corner post

Corner post

5'-0"

Eleva B

Corner post

The house on the hill

A perfect project for that first scratchbuilt wood structure

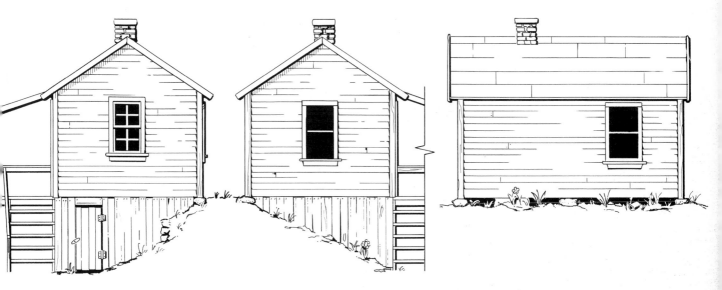

BY SAM SWANSON
PHOTOS BY THE AUTHOR

THIS HO scale house on the hill combines features of several working-class homes from the 1930s and will be a nice addition to the Cripple Creek Central layout. It's also a good choice for your first attempt at scratchbuilding with wood. Let's get right to it.

PREPARING THE WALLS

After collecting the materials and reading through the article once, cut out the wall templates in fig. 1 and trace them onto your sheet of clapboard siding. (Make a copy if you don't want to cut up your magazine.)

Cut the door and window openings halfway through. (Read the sidebar, "Working with wood," if you're unfamiliar with basic cutting techniques.) This will make the lines easier to find and finish cutting after you've painted.

Distress the walls, as shown in fig. 2, then stain them with a solution of 3 drops of India ink dissolved in 1 ounce of rubbing alcohol. A no. 4 flat brush works well and will cover three boards in one pass. Stain all the stripwood with this same ink solution.

Allow the walls to dry for about an hour, and then lightly sand individual boards with 320-grit sandpaper. Seal the walls with a thin coat of Testor's Dullcote. The sanding removes any wood fuzz that may result from the distressing, and the Dullcote seals the wood to minimize the amount of paint it absorbs.

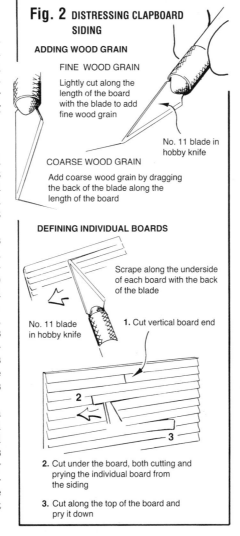

Fig. 2 DISTRESSING CLAPBOARD SIDING

ADDING WOOD GRAIN

FINE WOOD GRAIN

Lightly cut along the length of the board with the blade to add fine wood grain

No. 11 blade in hobby knife

COARSE WOOD GRAIN

Add coarse wood grain by dragging the back of the blade along the length of the board

DEFINING INDIVIDUAL BOARDS

Scrape along the underside of each board with the back of the blade

No. 11 blade in hobby knife

1. Cut vertical board end

2. Cut under the board, both cutting and prying the individual board from the siding

3. Cut along the top of the board and pry it down

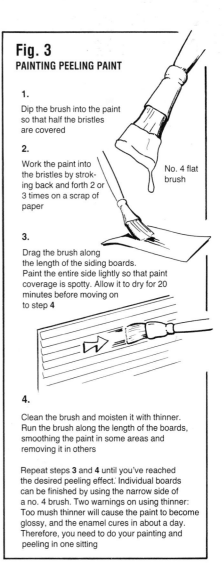

Fig. 3
PAINTING PEELING PAINT

1.
Dip the brush into the paint so that half the bristles are covered

2.
Work the paint into the bristles by stroking back and forth 2 or 3 times on a scrap of paper

No. 4 flat brush

3.
Drag the brush along the length of the siding boards. Paint the entire side lightly so that paint coverage is spotty. Allow it to dry for 20 minutes before moving on to step **4**

4.
Clean the brush and moisten it with thinner. Run the brush along the length of the boards, smoothing the paint in some areas and removing it in others

Repeat steps **3** and **4** until you've reached the desired peeling effect. Individual boards can be finished by using the narrow side of a no. 4 brush. Two warnings on using thinner: Too mush thinner will cause the paint to become glossy, and the enamel cures in about a day. Therefore, you need to do your painting and peeling in one sitting

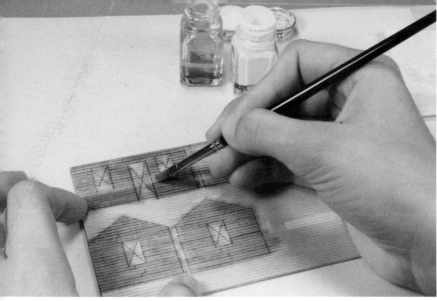

FIG. 4. DETAILING THE WALLS
Above left: The walls were stained with dilute India ink and allowed to dry; then they were lightly painted with Testor's FS Flat White enamel to represent faded and peeling paint. **Below right:** Openings were cut, and the door and windows were test-fit before the walls were cut out. **Above:** The walls were braced from behind with 1/8"-square stripwood.

WORKING WITH WOOD

CUTTING WOOD

- Use a no. 11 blade in a hobby knife or single-edge razor blade.
- Change blades often. Clean, precise cuts are easiest to make with new blades.
- Use a metal straightedge to guide the blade during long cuts. Also use it to cover the part you're cutting so an errant cut won't ruin the part's surface.
- Use a series of shallow strokes, rather than trying to cut through the wood in one sweep.

SANDING WOOD

- Use wet-or-dry sandpaper for fine grits of 240 or more. Wetting the wood often makes precision sanding easier.
- Sand along the wood grain where possible; always sand in the same direction rather than in circles.
- Keep the sandpaper flat by using a block of wood to back the paper, an emery board as bought, or a finer-grit sandpaper glued onto an emery board.

GLUING WOOD

- Use glue sparingly when joining two wood objects, but always coat both surfaces before pressing them together.
- When using any form of white glue, hold the glued joint firmly with your hands for 2 minutes. During this time, inspect the joint and overall alignment. Pick any glue that's oozed from the joint with the point of a no. 11 blade after the glue has started to set (when it has the consistency of putty).
- Where possible, weight the glued joint for at least 2 hours. If the pieces are badly warped, weight overnight.

Paint the walls with the same no. 4 brush. The technique used to represent peeling paint is shown in fig. 3. I used Testor's FS Flat White enamel, but you can use other readily available flat enamel colors from Pactra or Humbrol.

After the paint has dried, cut out the window and door openings (see fig. 4). Test-fit the window and door castings before cutting out the walls.

DETAILING AND ASSEMBLING WALLS

Prepare the plastic castings for painting by filing away any flash or sprue bumps and washing them in warm, soapy water. Paint the castings to match the walls, using flat enamel and thinner, and brushing with the wood grain. The light gray color of the Grandt Line parts aids in painting them to match the sides, so if you use other window and door castings, first paint them gray. Allow the painted castings to dry overnight.

After cutting the walls free, glue interior braces to the back of each and place them under several heavy books for at least 2 hours. (I use Elmer's Carpenter's Wood Glue for Darker Wood for wood-to-wood and wood-to-plastic joints, Elmer's Glue-All for window glazing, and Plastruct Plastic Weld Cement for plastic-to-plastic joints.)

Detail the walls by gluing in the windows and door frame, glazing and shading the windows, and cementing the corner posts onto the right and left sides.

I painted the doorknob and key plate with Testor's FS Flat Black, washed them with Polly S Rust, then cemented the door slightly ajar. A final light

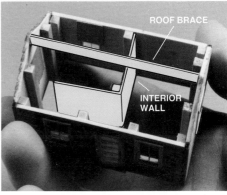

FIG. 5. ASSEMBLING THE WALLS
FIG. 5. ASSEMBLING THE WALLS
Left: Our author used graph paper to make sure the building came out square. **Above:** The roof brace and interior wall completed the assembly.

application of the ink solution, particularly on the underside of wall and window boards, ties the components of each wall together visually and helps the distressing stand out.

Using a piece of graph paper, test-fit the walls as shown in fig. 5. Lightly sand the edges and tack them together with tiny beads of white glue until they fit squarely with no large gaps. Before gluing the walls together permanently, check their vertical squareness with a drafting triangle.

Allow the assembled walls to dry for two hours, then add the roof brace and interior wall. I installed the wall so it's impossible to look all the way through the building. Stain the interior wall with ink solution.

THE ROOF

Trace the roof templates (fig. 1) onto the .040" sheetwood and cut out the three roof panels. Use the ink solution to stain the edges, the underside of the porch roof, and those underside portions of the main panels that will overhang the sides. Place the panels under a weight for an hour while drying.

Figure 6 shows how I made tar-paper roofing by painting a 4"-square piece of typing paper on both sides with Polly S

Grimy Black. Once the paper has dried, cut it into scale 24"-wide strips. Starting at the bottom of each house roof panel, spread glue along the back of each strip and press it onto the roof panel. Overlap the strips by a small amount — 1/32" is fine.

Glue the tar-papered house roof panels in place and add a ridge filler. I cut mine from the .040" sheet stock. Finish the house roof by folding a strip of tar paper in half lengthwise and gluing it over the peak.

Detail the roof by adding the chimney, repair patches, and dust and soot streaks. Then hollow out the chimney with a no. 11 blade and paint it with Floquil Primer. Before cementing it to the roof with two-part epoxy, carve out the portion of the roof peak for the chimney hole. After painting the bricks (I used shades of gray mixed from white and black flat enamel) and gluing the chimney in place, paint its inside flat black. Simulate the sealing tar around the chimney and roof patches with gloss black enamel, and the soot and dust streaks with black and gray chalk, respectively.

Finish the house by adding the roof fascia boards, which should be painted to match the siding and cut from the template in fig. 1.

THE BASE AND CELLAR

For the base, use a 3½" square of plywood that's at least 3/8" thick. Build the hill the house fits against with whatever material you like — I used four layers of 3/16"-thick foam core board (see fig. 7). After cutting the foam core to shape, I covered it with a 1/8"-thick layer of Durham's Water Putty, which I also used to sculpt the three flat stones the back of the house rests on.

Construct the top of the cellar frame, then add the two outer corner posts and fasten the frame temporarily to the bottom of the house with masking tape. Carve out depressions at the top of the hill for the three support stones, and adjust the stones and frame so the house rests level. Glue the stones and frame to the base with dark wood glue. Remove the house once the stones and framework have dried.

Build the rest of the cellar framework directly on the base. Paint the stones and add the retaining wall using 1/16"-square stripwood. Construct a posterboard dam around the base, as shown in fig. 7, then sprinkle on soil and use an eyedropper to bond it with a mixture of 1 part water, 1 part white glue, and a few drops of liquid dishwashing detergent. Just wet

FIG. 6. ADDING THE ROOF
Left: Tar-paper roofing was represented with strips of black-painted typing paper.
Above: Repairs give the roof a worn but well-maintained look. Drybrushing brings out details.

FIG. 7. ADDING THE CELLAR
Above: Our author butted his house up against a hill made from foam core board. **Right:** He temporarily taped on the house to level the floor frame. **Below left:** The timber frame was completed, then a cardboard dam held dirt in place while it was bonded with dilute white glue. **Below right:** As the final step, he applied the vertical boards individually.

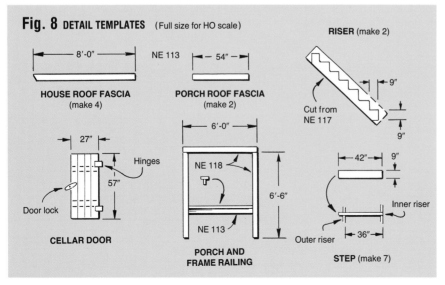

the soil — don't allow the solution to pool on the base.

Cut the cellar boards in various widths from the .020″ x 5/32″ stripwood, and glue them in place. Add the cellar door, along with its hinges and door stop, as shown in fig. 8.

Distress the cellar boards and door and add nail holes along the tops and bottoms, poking them in with a pin. As a way to simulate water damage caused by the cellar boards being in direct contact with the ground, touch the bottom of selected boards with a brushful of the ink solution. The stain will be drawn up into each board and realistically darken its lower half.

FINISHING THE MODEL

Glue the house atop the cellar frame and stones. Cut some more stripwood to

---

Fig. 8 DETAIL TEMPLATES (Full size for HO scale)

← 8'-0" → NE 113

HOUSE ROOF FASCIA
(make 4)

← 54" →

PORCH ROOF FASCIA
(make 2)

RISER (make 2)

9"

Cut from
NE 117

9"

27″

Hinges

57″

Door lock

CELLAR DOOR

← 6'-0" →

NE 118

6'-6"

NE 113

**PORCH AND
FRAME RAILING**

← 42″ → 9″

9″

Inner riser

Outer riser ← 36″ →

STEP (make 7)

Products used

Alexander Scale Models
2705 chimney

Evergreen Scale Models
9007 .015″ clear styrene

Floquil
110009 Primer

Grandt Line
5021 five-panel door
5030 27″ x 48″ double-hung windows
5095 plastic hinge assortment

Northeastern stripwood
111 .020″ x .040″ (1)
113 .020″ x 1/16″ (1)
115 .020″ x 3/32″ (1)
117 .020″ x 5/32″ (3)
157 .040″ x 2″ (1)
180 1/16″-square (2)
231 1/8″-square (1)
378 1/16″-square clapboard siding (1)

Polly S
410013 Grimy Black
410073 Rust

Testor
1260 Dullcote
1749 FS Flat Black enamel
1768 FS Flat White enamel

Miscellaneous
Durham's Water Putty
Elmer's Carpenter's Wood Glue for Darker Wood
Elmer's Glue-All
foam core board, 3/16″ thick
graph paper
India ink
liquid dishwashing detergent
Plastruct Plastic Weld Cement
plywood, 3/8″ thick
rubbing alcohol
two-part epoxy
typing paper

various widths, and add the porch floor. Then put on the remaining porch details. Build the frame from the template in fig. 7, and glue it in place at the same time you install the porch roof. Let the frame and roof dry for a couple hours and then tar-paper the porch roof.

Next, add the roof fascia and install the porch railing and stairs. An easy way to cut the stair risers is to cut out the template and tack-glue it on the stripwood. Cut the notches in the risers, then remove the paper template.

Build the stairs in place by first gluing on the inner and outer risers, adding the individual treads from top to bottom, and finishing with the railing. This sequence lets you make the stairs as rickety or as well-maintained as you want.

And now you've done it; you've constructed a model home. ✿

A. L. Schmidt

Cast-metal structures and details can be colorful additions to any layout. This Woodland Scenics gas station is the latest addition to our HO scale Cripple Creek Central beginners project.

A gas station for our HO project layout

The basics of working with cast-metal parts

BY JEFF WILSON

SHOW SOME modelers cast-metal parts and a file, and the next thing you'll have to do is coax them out from under their workbenches. For some reason, many modelers have developed an aversion to working with metal. They believe it's more difficult to work with, paint, and glue than other materials, namely plastic.

This month we'll try to dispel that notion. There are hundreds of cast-metal kits and detail parts available that, with a little work, can become focal points on a layout. So don't be afraid — just follow along as we tackle a project step by step. We chose a metal Woodland Scenics gas station kit to demonstrate the techniques of working with cast-metal parts.

BASICS OF CAST METAL

You probably already have many of the tools you need. Here's what I used: medium-size (8″) flat mill bastard file, set of needle files, and sharp hobby knife. Another handy tool is a file card, which is a small wire brush used to clean files. It's a good idea to have a separate set of files for metal work.

Begin as you would with any plastic kit. Spread out the parts and become familiar with them. As fig. 1 shows, this kit is fairly simple. The kit's gas pumps are the style used in the early 1900s, with the glass top that filled with gasoline. Since our HO scale Cripple Creek Central is set in more modern times, I chose to substitute a pair of

Columbia Valley 1950s pumps. Feel free to use whichever appeals to you.

Cast-metal parts usually have more flash (excess material along the mold parting lines) than do plastic ones. You can easily clean this up with your knife and files. Figure 2 shows how I began by using the large file to clean up the edges of the walls and roof sections. Use long, even strokes. The material comes off easily and quickly, so be careful not to remove too much. Test-fit the walls at each corner to ensure a good fit. If the walls are slightly warped, they can be bent back into shape with your hands.

Next, use needle files to clean up any smaller areas of flash, such as window frames and detail parts. A hobby knife is also handy for this.

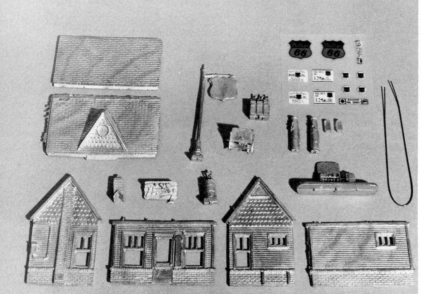

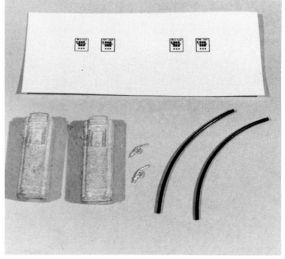

Fig. 1. The gas station kit is fairly simple. The building has four walls and two roof sections, and the kit includes several detail parts. The Columbia Valley gas pumps are also metal.

PAINTING

The next step is to prepare the parts for painting by using an old toothbrush to scrub them with soap and water. Rinse them under running water and let them air-dry. This gets rid of grease, oil, and filings that can prevent the paint from adhering to the metal.

Painting cast metal isn't that difficult. I painted everything using various sizes of brushes. I started by giving each part a coat of Floquil Earth. Unlike the Polly S paints we've been using, Floquil paints are solvent-based and their vapor is harmful. Do your painting in a well-ventilated area. I chose this paint because I've found Floquil holds onto metal very well, and Earth is a neutral color that provides a good base for other colors. Once this coat has dried, water-based Polly S (or other brand) paints can be used for subsequent colors. Let the Floquil paint dry for several days before proceeding to the next step.

I finished our kit with Polly S paints. The walls are Reefer White, with Caboose Red trim. I used Roof Brown for the roof and Brown for the brickwork. The detail parts were painted with several colors. Feel free to substitute other colors. The color photo gives you an idea of how the detail parts were painted. Once the building was assembled, I drybrushed some Earth on the roof.

ASSEMBLY

The Columbia Valley gas pumps include a length of black insulated wire for hoses. I substituted the wire from

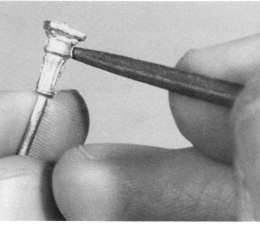

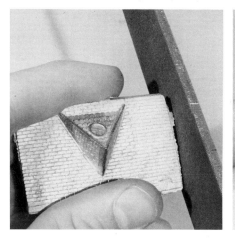

Fig. 2. Begin by using a large flat file to clean up the edges of the wall and roof sections. You can then use needle files and a hobby knife to remove flash from detail parts and window openings.

the Woodland Scenics kit because it's easier to work with. Drill no. 71 holes in the sides of the pumps to accept the hose and nozzle, and use cyanoacrylate adhesive (CA) to secure them in place. Once the CA had dried, I painted the hose black and the nozzle gray. Then, after adding the "This Sale" signs to the pump faces, I covered them with a two-part clear epoxy. This material nicely simulates the glass that's found on real pumps.

Figure 3 shows how the dry-transfer lettering is applied to the building, signs, and gas pumps.

The next step is to cut the clear acetate window material to size and glue it in place behind the windows with small drops of CA.

I also used CA to assemble the building. Use your knife to scrape any paint from the mating surfaces, and glue each corner by placing a few drops of CA along the mating edges. Press the pieces together firmly until the bond is secure and then let the joint dry for a few minutes. Do the same with the two roof halves.

ADDING THE SCENE TO THE LAYOUT

I planted the station next to Bob's Drug & Hobby. I used a technique similar to the one Jim Kelly used when adding that building in the October 1991 MR. Scrape away the existing scenicking material with a putty knife and add a patch of Sculptamold for the building and driveway areas. Cut bases for the building and pump island from .020″ styrene, and use Walthers Goo to glue them in place on the Sculptamold.

Next, paint the area with your flat tan latex paint and add scenicking material (I used Woodland Scenics no. 75 fine gray ballast for the drive and various shades of ground foam for the grassy areas). Affix this with a spray of diluted white or yellow glue, and use CA to glue the building and pump island into place.

Now you have another nice building on your layout, and you never have to fear metal castings again.

Next month Jim Kelly will add an industry to our branchline spur. He'll show you how to model a gravel pit that's not nearly as big as it looks. ☼

Products used
Columbia Valley
187 gas pumps

Floquil paint
110081 Earth

Polly S paint
410011 Reefer White
410012 Reefer Gray
410020 Caboose Red
410031 Reefer Yellow
410070 Roof Brown
410073 Rust
410082 Concrete
500103 Brown
501990 Bright Silver

Woodland Scenics
75 fine gray ballast
223 gas station

Miscellaneous
cyanoacrylate adhesive
flat tan latex paint
Goo adhesive
ground foam
Sculptamold
two-part epoxy
.020″ styrene

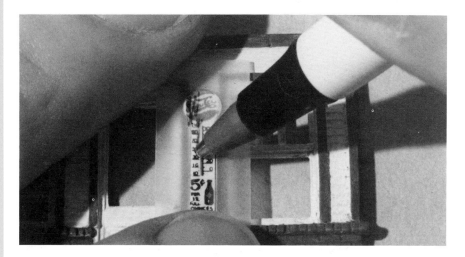

Fig. 3. To apply a dry transfer, hold the transfer in place and then, using a pen or burnishing tool, rub back and forth over it. Always rub in the same direction to avoid tearing the transfer.

Add a gravel pit to your layout

The old mirror trick adds depth to the scene

BY JIM KELLY

A. L. Schmidt

A mirror on the backdrop makes this quarry look larger than it is. One truck is a reflection of the other

THIS MONTH we're adding an industry to our HO scale beginner's layout. It's Olson's Quarry, named for our friend and notable model railroader, John. Maybe you can find a place for it on your own layout, even if you aren't building the Cripple Creek Central. Also, here's your chance to try the old mirror trick and see how you like it.

GOING TO IT

Consult the list of products used to see what you'll need. Step one was building the overhead bin from Faller's plastic kit. I used a hobby knife to cut the parts carefully from the sprues without damaging them. A 10″ flat file took care of any flash and burrs.

Assembly was with Testor's liquid plastic cement, applying it sparingly with an artist's brush and letting it flow into the joints. After it had dried completely, I cut out the base between the footings with a razor saw so the structure would straddle the track.

Next, I cut a big hole in that popcorn scenery that Jeff Wilson described building in the November 1991 issue of MR. A razor saw went through with ease.

I had a 5½″ x 15″ mirror cut at a mirror store and forked over 5 bucks for it. Using Walthers Goo I cemented it to our removable backdrop (see fig. 1).

To hide the top of the mirror I used one of the Faller overhead crane kits, modifying it as shown in fig. 2. Once these parts were firmly cemented to the backdrop and the mirror with Goo, I placed the backdrop back on the layout and rebuilt the scenery.

I rearranged the contours with Styrofoam popcorn, covered them with Rigid Wrap plaster-impregnated gauze. Then I added a layer of Sculptamold, following the same techniques described in the November issue.

Several days later, after the Sculptamold had dried, I scenicked the pit by painting it heavily with tan latex paint, then sprinkling on Highball's Light Brown Earth (fine) and several shades and textures of ground foam. The paint acts as an adhesive, but I also used dilute yellow glue, flowing it on with an eyedropper after the paint had set.

The other overhead crane kit was used to connect the conveyor on the backdrop with the loading bin. Just build it as per the kit directions, let the cement dry thoroughly, and cut it to a length that works with your setup.

REINFORCING THE ILLUSION

I used clumps of lichen to hide the edges of the mirror. Lichen, incidentally, is one of the oldest scenery materials, but still one of the best. The key to using it as bushes is clipping off the coarsest parts and using only fine tips. (You can salvage the best of the coarse material by cementing it to the layout

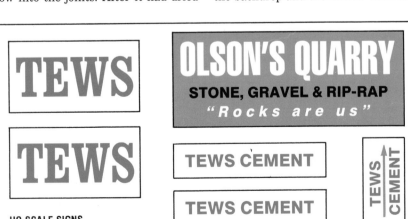

TEWS

TEWS

OLSON'S QUARRY
STONE, GRAVEL & RIP-RAP
"Rocks are us"

TEWS CEMENT

TEWS CEMENT

TEWS CEMENT

HO SCALE SIGNS

Fig. 1. BACKDROP. We cemented a mirror to the backdrop we described making in the July and November 1991 issues.

spraying it with an adhesive, and sprinkling on ground foam.)

Also, I tried to arrange clumps of lichen in front of the mirror in ways that would draw the viewer's attention forward. A few tiny clumps along the bottom of the mirror helped break up the straight line there.

Painting the structure and adding a sign also helped pull attention forward. I brush-painted the bin portion with Polly S Dark Green, dipping the brush in water occasionally as I went along. Then I painted the footings with Earth.

To the rest of the structure I applied a wash of Roof Brown. This is accomplished by dipping the brush into the paint, then into water, and letting it flow down over the surface. In this procedure the paint often beads. To make it flow, just dip the tip of the brush into a drop of dishwashing detergent.

The clouds were another ploy to divert attention away from the mirror. They were brush-painted with Polly S Reefer White, and I tried to keep them small and simple.

Two last tricks saved the day. First, I painted the backdrop immediately above the conveyor with the same ground color used in the pit so that the pit appears to extend beyond it.

The second gambit was suggested by Art Curren and worked great. Art recommended painting a line or two on the floor of the pit and parallel with the point between the pit and the mirror. This would give several lines to look at, and the eye wouldn't go directly to the point. I tried it, using Polly S Roof Brown, and it worked. Thanks, Art.

So how does the old mirror trick work here? Pretty well, I'd say, and a heck of a lot better than if I had tried to paint a continuation of the gravel pit on the backdrop.

Well, that's it for this month. Join us next time when Bob Hayden trucks in a rock cliff made at his workbench. ⚙

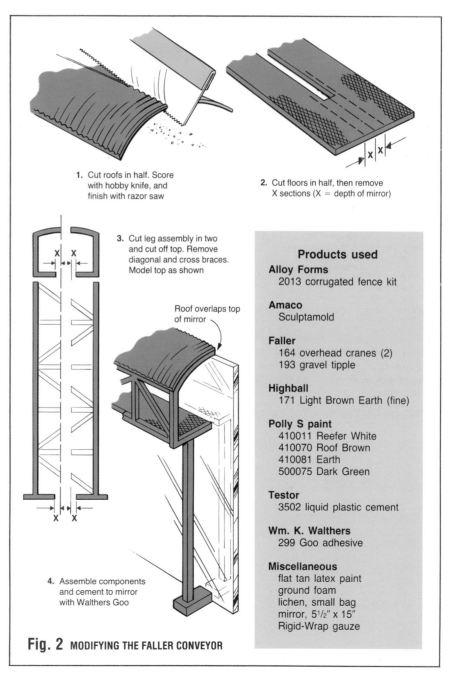

1. Cut roofs in half. Score with hobby knife, and finish with razor saw

2. Cut floors in half, then remove X sections (X = depth of mirror)

3. Cut leg assembly in two and cut off top. Remove diagonal and cross braces. Model top as shown

Roof overlaps top of mirror

4. Assemble components and cement to mirror with Walthers Goo

Fig. 2 MODIFYING THE FALLER CONVEYOR

Products used

Alloy Forms
2013 corrugated fence kit

Amaco
Sculptamold

Faller
164 overhead cranes (2)
193 gravel tipple

Highball
171 Light Brown Earth (fine)

Polly S paint
410011 Reefer White
410070 Roof Brown
410081 Earth
500075 Dark Green

Testor
3502 liquid plastic cement

Wm. K. Walthers
299 Goo adhesive

Miscellaneous
flat tan latex paint
ground foam
lichen, small bag
mirror, 5½" x 15"
Rigid-Wrap gauze

Rolling green hills in rural settings and town scenes such as this add to the diversity of the Cripple Creek Central.

A. L. Schmidt

Bob's Rock is the scenic highlight of our Cripple Creek Central, an HO layout we began building in the January 1991 issue. The cliff was built on the workbench, then installed in the layout.

Especially for beginners

Making rocks at the workbench

The joys of rock casting without the mess

BY BOB HAYDEN

PHOTOS BY THE AUTHOR

SOMETHING didn't look right to me on the rural side of our HO scale Cripple Creek Central layout. Then it struck me: The big hillside that Jim Kelly had built in the November 1991 issue was just too plain — it needed a rock face to give it character.

Now a time-honored technique for making rock faces is to make a rubber mold from a real rock. Then you pour plaster into it and slap it on the layout. Satisfying but messy, and messy is verboten on the Cripple Creek.

I reckoned that we could still use the rock-casting technique, if we did the messy parts away from the layout.

"Saw me out a chunk of that hillside," I told Jim, "and I'll make it into a snappy rock face you can install back into the layout without much fuss. I'll handle the sloppy parts on the picnic table in my backyard."

A HOLE IN A HILL

Winter came early, so actually I made the rock face in my basement. But I did avoid making much of a mess, and so can you. Molding and coloring the rock face is a good one-evening project, and installing it back in the layout is good for another evening. If you're like me, that's about a week's worth of model railroading!

Jim took the first step and the most

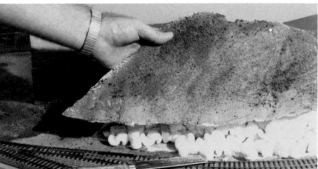

Fig. 1. CUTTING OUT THE HILLSIDE. Now you see it, now you don't. This chunk of hill was sawed out so Bob could take it home with him and add rocks. By golly, that Styrofoam popcorn we used to support the scenery shell in the November 1991 MR is still under there.

61

Products used

Amaco
41821 Sculptamold

Color-Rite
805 3½″ x 8″ rock mold
807 3½″ x 4¾″ rock mold

Polly S paint
410011 Reefer White

Miscellaneous
black India ink
flat tan latex paint
plaster of paris
plastic mixing bowl
rubber spatula
spray bottles (2)

Fig. 2. ROCK-MAKING TOOLS. Everything you need is shown here. Hardy souls can make their own molds by brushing liquid latex on rock faces. It takes half a dozen coats of rubber.

difficult one: He cut a two-foot section out of the beautiful hill he'd built only a few months earlier. See fig. 1. A razor saw sliced through the Sculptamold and plaster bandage scenery as nice as you please, and he presented me with a tidy, oblong-shaped chunk of the layout, which I took home.

I sawed about 1½″ off the flat bottom edge of the hillside, figuring I'd need that much clearance for the completed rock face to fit back into the hole.

The next step was to find the tools and materials needed to make the rocks. See fig. 2. The rock molds came from the hobby shop, and I tracked down the plaster of paris at a hardware store.

The earth-colored paint used on the rocks is the same latex used to color the rest of the scenery, but you'll also need a bottle of black India ink and some Polly S Reefer White.

The tools are real simple: a brush, artist's palette knife, rubber spatula, and a couple of hardware-store spray bottles. You'll also need something to mix plaster in. I used a plastic margarine tub. To minimize the mess as well as the cleanup, you will need two days' worth of newspapers.

FRESHER IS BETTER

The most important ingredient — heck, about the only ingredient is the plaster of paris. Like vegetables, it has to be fresh. If it's old, you run the risk of it taking a long time to set, or not setting at all, so buy a new supply especially for this project.

Spread out the newspapers four or five layers thick, and prop up the soon-to-be-rocky hillside on a couple of scraps of wood. Wet two of the rock molds by holding them under warm running water, then prop them face up and level next to the hillside. (Don't try to work with more than two molds at a time, unless you have more than two hands.)

Mix up a batch of plaster by pouring 1 measure of warm water into your mixing bowl, then adding 2 measures of plaster. I used a pair of 5-ounce waxed

Dixie cups as measures. Gently blend the plaster with the water until the mixture is smooth, then let it sit about 3 minutes while you size up where you want to place your first two molds.

Pour the plaster into the molds, filling each, as shown in fig. 3. Leave each mold alone for about 5 minutes and the plaster starts to set. While you wait, spray the hillside liberally with water so it won't draw moisture out of the plaster.

The mold is ready to apply to the scenery when you can pick it up and tilt it from side to side without the plaster running out. Also, when you squeeze it, gently the plaster wrinkles slightly.

Hold the loaded mold in the palm of your hand and gently but firmly press it into the scenery until a small amount of plaster is forced out from under the edges of the mold. Do the same with the second mold. Now hold both in place with your hands, making them conform to the contours beneath them for about 3 minutes or until you're sure they won't pull away on their own.

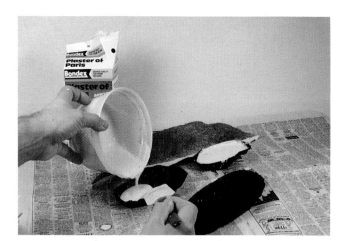

Fig. 3. POURING PLASTER. Plaster is poured into the mold and begins to set. Wetting the mold first helps the plaster seek the details.

Fig. 4. PLACING MOLDS. The molds are pressed in place and left until the plaster is firm. If removed too soon, detail might be damaged.

Fig. 5. BLACK MISTING. Spraying on dilute India ink brings out the detail. Don't worry about the darkness. The color will lighten as it dries.

Fig. 6. COLOR MIST. Dilute tan was sprayed on carefully to preserve the ink effects. The entire rock-painting session took 5 minutes.

If the phone hasn't rung, you can now leave the molds in place for about 15 minutes, as shown in fig. 4. Meanwhile, clean up your mixing bowl and spatula and measure the ingredients for the next batch.

Pry gently at the edges of a mold to make sure it will pull away cleanly from the plaster. (Because they're so rugged no harm is done in leaving the Color-Rite molds on the plaster for a half-hour or more.) Peel the molds off the cast rock faces and admire your work.

Repeat the molding, overlapping the castings, until you've covered the whole rock face. Where the castings meet you'll want to chip away at the plaster to blend the faces. Do this immediately after peeling away the molds. Use an old hobby knife or palette knife, and be sure to pry and chip at the plaster instead of cutting so the areas look like rock texture. It takes all of 30 seconds to get the hang of this.

COLORING WITH MIST

Now comes the fun part. Painting the rock face will take a grand total of 5 minutes — and that's if you dawdle. We'll do it while the rock castings are still damp from molding. Because they're still full of water, they won't absorb much color, and that's just what we want. (If you can't color the rocks immediately after molding, wet the castings again before coloring by spraying them with water until they won't absorb anymore.)

Mix the coloring solutions in two pump-type sprayer bottles. (You can also use window cleaner bottles.) Make a dark spray by combining ½ teaspoon of black India ink with 1 pint of water, and an earth spray by diluting 1 part of flat tan latex paint with 9 parts water. Add 3 or 4 drops of liquid dishwashing detergent to each spray bottle to make the liquids flow better.

Prop the rock face up at the same angle it will stand on the layout, and mist all of it with the India ink solution, as shown in fig. 5. Use plenty and let the excess run down over the rock face and settle in cracks.

As soon as you apply the ink wash, the rock face will come to life, and you'll be able to see all the detail. Don't worry that the color is too dark — it will lighten as it dries.

Follow up by misting on the earth spray, as shown in fig. 6. Go lightly with this. You don't want to cover up all the dark wash, especially in cracks and crevices. If you overdo the earth color, spray on more ink wash, then try again with a light spray of earth wash. Now clean up the mess, leaving the rock face propped up overnight to dry.

From this point the project became really easy for me, because I gave the cast rock face to Jim and let him take it from there. He glued the cliff in place with white glue and then worked the ground back in around the edges with Sculptamold. Next came the tan paint and various shades and textures of ground foam that we've been using on this layout.

I slipped back in at the end and drybrushed the rocks to add highlights and bring out the detail. See fig. 7. Other finishing touches could include a few sprigs of lichen to simulate weeds clinging tenaciously to the rock face, a trickle of gloss medium to represent water leaking down in a place or two, and perhaps a touch of spray-can graffiti like my "Class of 77" marking, done with a colored pencil.

Meanwhile we've heard lots of sawing, hammering, and a little cussing coming from the direction of Gordy's Pond. Read all about it next month when a tar-paper shack is added to the layout. ⬦

Fig. 7. DRYBRUSHING. After the rock was installed on the layout it took a week to dry. Then Bob drybrushed it with Polly S Reefer White to bring out the detail. He dips the tip of the brush in paint, pulls it through a paper towel to remove nearly all the paint, and strokes the rocks lightly.

FRONT

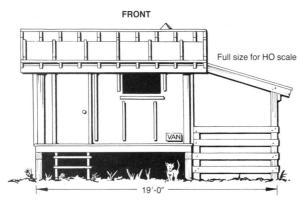

Full size for HO scale

VAN

|← 19'-0" →|

This month we add a peaceful little shack to one corner of our HO scale beginners' layout.

A tar paper shack for your layout

LEFT SIDE

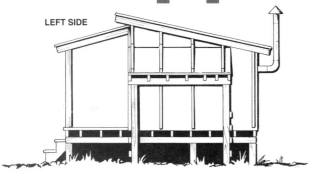

REAR

9'-3"

RIGHT SIDE

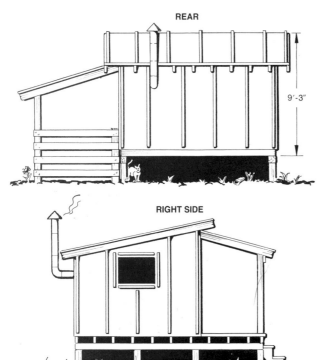

|← 14'-9" →|

This HO hideaway will give you a good introduction to scratchbuilding

BY BILL MORRISSEY
PHOTOS BY A. L. SCHMIDT

NEARLY every model railroad has a corner toward the back that seems to be wasted space. On my own layout I try to have an interesting vignette wherever a visitor might look. For our HO scale Cripple Creek Central I came up with this shack for one of those odd corners. It's a simple tar paper shanty that could be a hunting shack, a weekend retreat, or most anything. The design and construction are simple, and it makes a nice one- or two-evening project.

A shack like this shouldn't be too large, just room enough for a stove, a table, some chairs, a couple bunks, and maybe a storage cabinet — 10 x 12 feet is plenty. For a foundation some cedar posts about 6 feet apart will raise the floor off the ground and provide sanctuary from the skunks and snakes. Any more-or-less level spot will provide an adequate site.

CONSTRUCTION

Study fig. 1 and start by cutting the floor from .020"-thick scribed styrene sheet. To cut styrene just score it with a hobby knife, then snap it along the line. The scribed lines should run from front to back, as they will show on the porch floor.

Add the 2 x 6 floor joists, spacing them 18" apart. I don't try to cut parts like these joists exactly to size — they're difficult to install precisely. Instead, I cut them too long and trim them flush after the cement has dried. Add two 6 x 6s under the ends of the joists as foundation timbers. Use a liquid cement for plastics and flow it into the joints with an artist's brush.

Consulting fig. 1 again, cut each of the walls from .020" styrene sheet (plain or scribed, it doesn't matter), cutting out the window and door openings as you go.

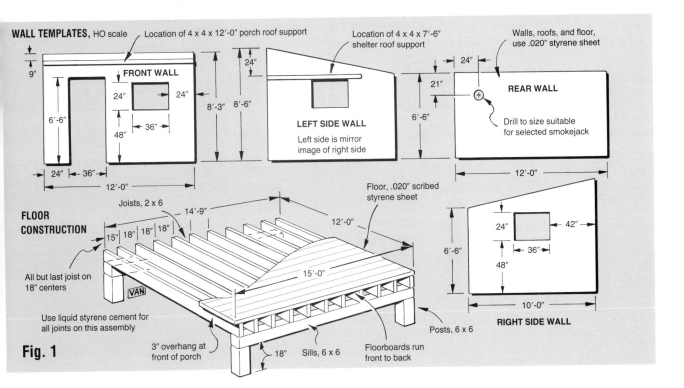

WALL TEMPLATES, HO scale

Location of 4 x 4 x 12'-0" porch roof support

FRONT WALL

9"
6'-6"
24" | 24"
48"
36"
24" | 36"
12'-0"
8'-3" | 8'-6"

Location of 4 x 4 x 7'-6"
shelter roof support

LEFT SIDE WALL

Left side is mirror
image of right side

24"
6'-6"

Walls, roofs, and floor,
use .020" styrene sheet

24"
21"

REAR WALL

Drill to size suitable
for selected smokejack

6'-6"
12'-0"

FLOOR CONSTRUCTION

Joists, 2 x 6
14'-9"
15" | 18" | 18" | 18"
All but last joist on
18" centers
VAN
Use liquid styrene cement for
all joints on this assembly

Floor, .020" scribed
styrene sheet
12'-0"
15'-0"

3" overhang at
front of porch
18"
Sills, 6 x 6
Floorboards run
front to back
Posts, 6 x 6

RIGHT SIDE WALL

24" | 42"
36"
48"
6'-6"
10'-0"

Fig. 1

Add the door to the front wall before cementing it to the floor. See fig. 2. Cross-bracing on the door is optional — it could be hidden on the inside. The porch and shelter roof supports should also be added before the walls are assembled to the floor (fig. 1).

Install the back wall first. Each wall should cover the edge of the floor sheet, but you want to leave those neat joist ends exposed. Add scraps of styrene to reinforce the joints as you go. Figure 2 illustrates the reinforcement principle.

The side walls are added next, overlapping the rear wall where the corners meet. Last, install the front wall, fitting it between and flush with the front edges of the side walls.

ADDING THE TAR PAPER

Use typing paper to simulate tar paper — it has just enough surface texture to be effective. A rubber cement works well for bonding paper to plastic. Make sure that the cement covers the entire wall you're doing, or the paper is likely to bubble and become uneven at a later time.

After the cement has dried, trim the paper flush with the edges of the walls and the door and window openings. If you get any rubber cement in unwanted places, let it dry thoroughly and rub it off with a pencil eraser or your fingertip.

Add the roof and paper it; paint the paper black. Tar paper weathers quickly, so I used Floquil Grimy Black. While the paint was drying I prepainted the 1 x 2 battens that hold the tar paper in place. All the "exposed wood" on this shack is unpainted, so I used a shade of gray.

UNDERSTANDING BATTENS

It's hard to give specific directions for positioning the battens, so I'll explain the general principles and leave the details to you.

Tar paper comes in 36"-wide rolls and is applied with a small (3" to 6") overlap. It's held down with roofing nails. Exposed edges are vulnerable to wind damage, so they're reinforced by nailing on strips of wood called battens. These are 1 x 2s or smaller. Since the sheets overlap, the distance between battens is about 32". Battens are also applied wherever the tar paper goes around a corner and around door and window openings.

The battens on our shack shouldn't be too neatly applied. This is a shack, remember? Leave gaps between battens, and perhaps one or two should not be exactly square. Attach your plastic battens to the painted bond paper with cyanoacrylate adhesive (CA). Rubber cement is too messy for this fine work.

We made our small backdrop by cutting some trees from a Detail Associates no. 7511 paper backdrop and cementing them to a piece of cardboard with a spray photomounting adhesive.

DETAILS

Start by adding the 2 x 4 rafter ends to the front edge of the roof, again cutting them a little long and trimming them flush later. Next, cement the porch posts to the roof support (fig. 2) and set it aside to dry. Cut out the porch roof and use liquid styrene cement to fasten it to the front wall. While the joint is still somewhat flexible, slip the support post assembly in place and apply styrene cement. Then, while these joints are still soft, shift the parts back and forth until the posts are vertical and everything lines up.

Now go ahead and make the outside storage shelter roof and supports the same way. After the cement holding these parts has dried, add the side fences to the shelter enclosure.

Add tar paper and battens to the roofs. The tar paper would be rolled over the edges of the roof for a couple of inches, so paint the roof edges black while you're painting the roof paper.

The front porch steps appear to be a tedious chore, but it's just a matter of adding one piece to the next. Besides, these steps don't have to be a masterpiece of precision since this shack wouldn't have been built by professionals.

Try this trick: Using rubber cement, secure the backs of the two step supports to a piece of paper. That way they will stay put while you cement the treads in place.

Add the rafters along the sides and the false rafter ends along the edges of the various roofs. Then install the smokejack on the rear wall and paint it black. I made mine out of plastic rod, but Campbell has good plastic smokejacks.

Next come the three shutters, although actually the one on the right side is the only one that will show — the other two are up under the porch and shelter roofs. Don't forget to cover the shutters with tar paper too!

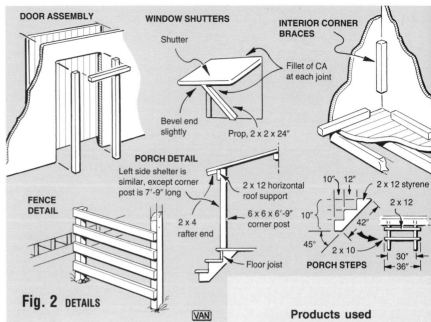

Fig. 2 DETAILS

Paint all the remaining unpainted styrene parts. Use a fine-point brush and the same paint you used for the battens. Any little mistakes can be touched up with the black paint.

I weathered my cabin with brown chalk, since tar paper fades to an irregular dark brownish color as it gets old. Just grind a pastel chalk stick on sandpaper to make a little pile of chalk, then brush it on. Next came tan and gray weathering chalk, concentrating it on the lower walls to represent an accumulation of dirt.

Let your imagination roll with the details: maybe a stack of firewood, a garbage can or two, an outhouse, a flower bed, even a bearskin tacked to the wall. Add some brush and weeds, and you've created that perfect little weekend hideaway. ☼

Products used
Evergreen styrene
2050 .020" V-groove siding
8102 HO 1 x 2 strip
8104 HO 1 x 4 strip
8204 HO 2 x 4 strip
8206 HO 2 x 6 strip
8210 HO 2 x 10 strip
8212 HO 2 x 12 strip
8404 HO 4 x 4 strip
8606 HO 6 x 6 strip
9020 .020" sheet

Floquil paint
110012 Reefer Gray
110013 Grimy Black

Miscellaneous
pastel chalks
rubber cement
typing paper

NORTH STAR TENT CO.

HO SCALE SIGNS

mine flush, so I modified them as shown in fig. 3. You'll have just enough plugs, provided you don't plug the upper left window on the left end wall (as I did). Use a window casting there instead.

Last I added the fire escapes. These are tedious to build and you could just leave them off. I think they're really neat, though, and a detail not often seen on models.

THE OFFICE

The little office on the left side of the building called for a lot of cutting and fitting, as shown in fig. 4. Again, you could leave it off and still have a nice building. I swapped some long and short windows around on my model, but it wasn't worth it so I recommend you don't bother.

Once you've cemented the office to the main building, you can weather them both. I mixed a half-dozen drops of India ink with several cups of water, added a few drops of dishwashing detergent, and sprayed this solution on

the model with a spray bottle. The effect was miraculous. Presto — we went from shiny plastic to a building that looked like it had been around awhile.

The roofs on my building are just 1/16″-illustration board, with styrene strips cemented across the back to represent the tops of the rear walls. See fig. 5. I painted these with Polly S 500874 Brown to match the walls. (Polly S has several browns, so you need to watch the number.)

You've got lots of roof details in your two Model Power kits, so have a ball — glue some on.

NEW AND BLUE

The new, drive-in portion of our building is made from Pikestuff's no. 5000 enginehouse. Step one is to install the doors and windows. Since the instructions are quite good, I won't interfere. You'll find Pikestuff's plastic is pretty tough stuff, so be patient, change the blades in your hobby knife now and then, and stick with it.

Once this addition was completed, I weathered it by flowing on Polly S 500060 Khaki, using a large soft brush, plenty of water, and a little dishwashing detergent to make the paint flow instead of bead up. Judge for yourself, but I really like the result.

I cemented the addition to the old building with CA (cyanoacrylate adhesive), then ran a bead of this same cement along the seam between the addition's roof and the old wall. This I painted black to represent tar.

Last I glazed the windows, then installed rear walls made from illustration board. These block the view so we don't look through the building to our backdrop. They also help prevent the roofs from sagging.

And there you have it. I wouldn't want to kid you. This is not a real easy project, more like medium difficulty. Plan on four or five evenings to complete it.

Join us next time for our big reforestation project. We'll look at easy-to-build tree kits and add some to the layout. ✿

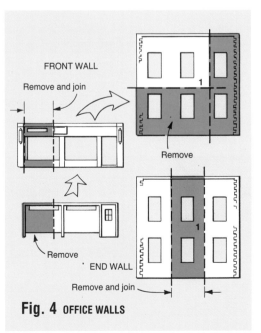

Fig. 4 OFFICE WALLS

FRONT WALL

Remove and join

Remove

1

Remove

END WALL

Remove and join

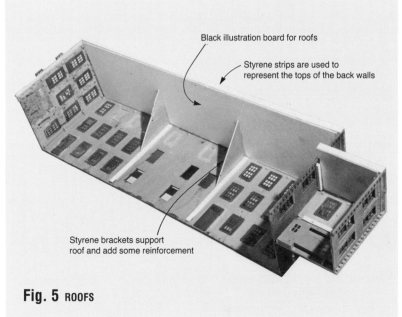

Fig. 5 ROOFS

Black illustration board for roofs

Styrene strips are used to represent the tops of the back walls

Styrene brackets support roof and add some reinforcement

Move over, Sherwood

We have a ball adding Woodland Scenics trees to the layout

Some store-bought trees are too perfect

Hack 'em up with scissors and pull off some foliage

Trees made with coarse lichen can be improved by spraying with adhesive and lightly sifting on some ground foam

Fig. 1
IMPROVING STORE-BOUGHT TREES

BY JIM KELLY
PHOTOS BY A. L. SCHMIDT

NOTHING DRESSES up a model railroad like trees. A well-done tree can be an interesting scene by itself, or you can use clumps or rows of trees to divide scenes from one another. We all like to play peekaboo with the trains as they go through or behind trees.

Plenty of model tree products are

Fig. 2. KIT ASSSEMBLY. Each tree comes as a flat plastic casting.

Bend the limbs to make the trees three-dimensional.

Our Atlas S-2 switcher rolls through the newly planted woods on the HO scale Cripple Creek Central RR.

Products used

Hobsco (Walthers)
299 Goo adhesive

Woodland Scenics
M125 paint set
TR1102 realistic tree kit
TR1103 realistic tree kit

Miscellaneous
Matte medium

Some of the better ready-to-plant trees and kits come from Kibri, Heki, and Faller. We've been adding some of those to our HO scale project layout as we've gone along.

THE NEW WOODLAND SCENICS KITS

For this month's story we tried a new tree product and came away extremely enthusiastic. Woodland Scenics has introduced a new line of tree kits that just may revolutionize this phase of the hobby. Look at our lead photo and judge for yourself.

The sequence of how-to photos (fig. 2) shows how these are put together. These aren't just shake-the-box jobs — figure 10 to 30 minutes per tree, depending on how big it is. The price is reasonable, and the plastic trunks offer several big advantages — they hold the shape you bend them to and are unbreakable. They have a tremendous advantage over dried weeds in that regard.

The trunks have realistic bark detail molded in, and as our photos show, you can bring this out by drybrushing. Just dip your brush (a 1/4" flat is good) in the paint, then stroke most of it off on a paper towel. Brush lightly on the tree

available, and that's a good thing because it's virtually impossible to have too many trees on a layout. Also we need a large variety, just because that's how Nature does it. At the hobby shop you'll find trees in both ready-to-plant and kit forms. Some of these are quite nice, some are, shall we say, a tad less than convincing. Let your eyesight be your judge.

Figure 1 shows some tricks for improving some of the less-than-successful store-bought trees. Often the more bilious-

colored trees can be improved by spraying them with more natural colors from a spray can. Make sure you do any spraying outdoors and use an acrylic. Solvent-based paints will dissolve some of the foams used in making trees.

Meanwhile, lots of modelers make their own trees, often using dried weeds. If you'd like to read some good articles on scratchbuilding trees, allow me to recommend one of our books, *Scenery Tips and Techniques*.

Drybrush the trunk to bring out bark detail.

Apply Goo, a rubber-based adhesive, to the branches.

Drybrushing the bark makes these trees look good enough to stand alone in the foreground.

SELECTION GUIDE						
	Item	Actual Height	Trees Per Package	Scale Height		
				N 1/160	HO 1/87	O 1/48
Deciduous Trees	TR1101	3/4" - 3"	36	10' - 40'	5' - 22'	3' - 12'
	TR1102	3" - 5"	14	40' - 67'	22' - 36'	12' - 20'
	TR1103	5" - 7"	7	67' - 93'	36' - 51'	20' - 28'
Evergreen Trees	TR1104	2 1/2" - 4"	42	33' - 53'	18' - 29'	10' - 16'
	TR1105	4" - 6"	24	53' - 80'	29' - 44'	16' - 24'
	TR1106	6" - 8"	16	80' - 106'	44' - 58'	16' - 24'

trunk, and a trace of the small amount of paint left in the brush will transfer to only the high spots.

We did our highlighting with the Woodland Scenics paint set no. M125, which gives you 12 colors for $3.95. These cover well and clean up with water.

Walthers Goo worked well for attaching the foliage. The instructions call for a contact cement, but a phone call to Woodland Scenics revealed that they use Goo. Three bags of foliage material (light, medium, and dark green) come with each kit, and I used no more than half of it. The leftover material is excellent for bushes, and our layout photo shows how we used some that way.

After attaching the foliage to the branches, we sprayed the trees with dilute matte medium. This is a clear acrylic varnish sold at art supply stores. It dries to a flat (that's why they call it matte) finish. We mix it about 6 parts water to 1 part adhesive and spray it on with an inexpensive household sprayer. (Spray lots of soap and water through the sprayer after using it to prevent clogging.)

If you're not inclined to mix your own adhesive, Woodland Scenics offers a Scenic Cement (no. S191) that's ready to go. They even have a sprayer (no. S192) to use for applying it.

Each Woodland Scenics tree kit costs $11.95, and the number of trees you get depends on their height. Both deciduous (like those we used) and pine trees are available, and as the chart shows, you can use these trees in a variety of scales.

Woodland Scenics offers these same trees ready-built, but you can save 50 to 75 percent by making them yourself. If you do use some of the ready-built trees, you can improve them a lot by drybrushing the trunks.

It's not often we devote a feature article to so much discussion of a new product, but you're going to love these trees.

Be sure to join us next month when we add a working crossing signal. ◘

Add the clumps of foliage.

Fix the foliage by spraying with dilute matte medium.

Our friendly brakeman will wave at both man and beast. We began building this HO scale beginners' layout in the January 1991 issue. The tunnel entrance is hand-carved, using Polyterrain Mud. The cows are drinking at a spring made with Polyterrain water gel.

Add a tunnel to your layout

Build a hill quick with chunks of foam

BY JIM KELLY

PHOTOS BY A. L. SCHMIDT

"YOU KNOW WHAT this layout needs?" says my old pal Charlie.

"No," says I, "but I'll bet you're going to tell me."

"Well," he says, "I wouldn't give you two cents for a model railroad that didn't have a tunnel!"

Hmmm. Now I've seen lots of layouts that didn't have tunnels, but at the same time I thought old Charlie had a point. Bridges and tunnels are two things most beginners want to try right away. We like to watch a train go through, behind, or into something.

Besides, I'd been assigned the job of reviewing Polyterrain's scenery products, so I needed to build a scenic wonder of some sort. Here was a chance to swat two jobs with a single slab of extruded foam.

BASIC SCENERY FORM

One thing you need before you can build a tunnel is something for the tunnel to go through, say a mountain or at least a good-sized hill. As I and others pondered the HO scale Cripple Creek Central, we could see that the rocks Bob Hayden had built (April 1992 MR) suggested a rocky ridge that could be continued across the layout. It would yield two interesting scenes: a notch for trains to pass through going up the quarry spur and a tunnel on the main line.

Snooping here and there about the building I discovered two fair-sized chunks of extruded foam insulation, one pink and one blue. I started breaking off small (hand-sized) pieces and stacking them up to form the ridge, as seen in fig. 1.

I kept rearranging the pieces until I was satisfied with the form, then I draped it with Rigid-Wrap. This is a

73

Our new hill, right, looks like a natural extension of the rocks Bob Hayden built for our April story. We cast the rocks in plaster, then sprayed them with a dilute solution of black followed by a dilute solution of tan.

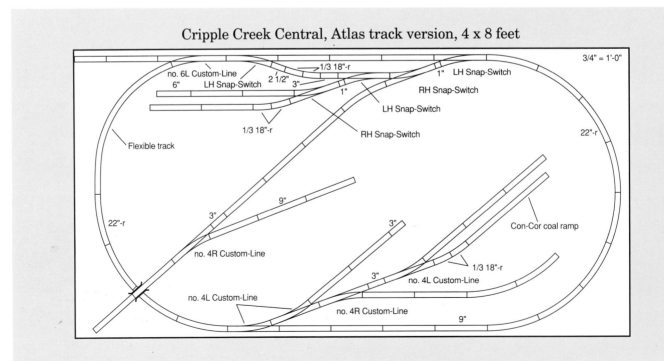

Cripple Creek Central, Atlas track version, 4 x 8 feet

3/4" = 1'-0"

no. 6L Custom-Line
6"   LH Snap-Switch

2 1/2"   3"

1/3 18"-r

1"   LH Snap-Switch

1"

RH Snap-Switch

LH Snap-Switch

Flexible track

1/3 18"-r

RH Snap-Switch

22"-r

22"-r

9"

3"

Con-Cor coal ramp

no. 4R Custom-Line

3"

1/3 18"-r

no. 4L Custom-Line

3"

no. 4L Custom-Line

no. 4R Custom-Line

9"

Fig. 1. SHAPING THE HILL. We built the contours of our new hill by breaking off chunks of foam insulation board (available at building centers) and stacking them until we had a shape we liked.

laster bandage material that you dip n water and place in position. Once it as dried, you have a hard scenic shell.

To smooth the hill I applied a top oat of Sculptamold, a papier-mache-ype product that's easy and neat to vork with. Just apply it quickly with a utty knife, then use a wetted 1" paint-rush to work and smooth it.

FINISHED SCENERY

Figure 2 shows the initial applica-ion of Polyterrain Mud used to model ocks around the tunnel portal. This dries very slowly, so you have plenty of time to carve and shape it. I then painted it with Polyterrain's acrylic paints.

The rocks on the back side of the hill were cast in place, using molding plaster in rubber molds and following the directions in Bob's article.

To finish the hill I painted it with tan latex paint, then sprinkled on various shades and textures of Woodland Scenics ground foam while the paint was still wet. To finish bonding the materials I sprayed on matte medium, diluted 6:1 with water and laced with a few drops of liquid dishwashing detergent.

Now came a favorite part of any project, standing back and admiring the results. The new ridge really did add a lot. Whereas the diagonal back-drop had divided the layout into two scenes, the hill now divided the rural side yet again. It made the layout look larger and more interesting.

"Know what the layout needs now?" asked Charlie.

"No," I said — wearily.

"Nuthin," he roared, "it looks just great!" ✿

uilt our layout with Kato's ck, but here by popular de-is a version using Atlas components. Sorry, but one of flexible track will have to ted in.

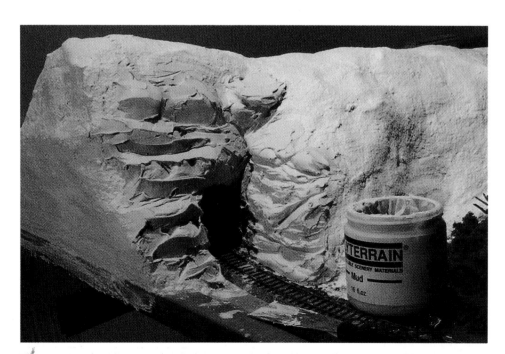

Fig. 2. MODELING ROCKS. We established rough forms with Polyterrain's Mud, then carved in nooks and crannies as it dried. Tiny cracks dry into the finished surfaces and add to the realism.

Grade-crossing action for your layout in a flash

Push-button control makes it simple

The citizens of Cripple Creek can breathe a little easier knowing that they'll be warned of oncoming trains before they breeze through the Main St. crossing next to the station.

BY KEITH THOMPSON
PHOTOS BY A. L. SCHMIDT

THIS MONTH we'll add crossing signals to our HO scale Cripple Creek Central beginners' layout using an off-the-shelf flasher circuit and Oregon Rail Supply's crossing flashers. The plastic lives you save may be your own.

I can hear you mumbling, "I don't know anything about electronics." Using ready-to-go circuitry, a 9-volt battery, and a push-button switch makes it easy.

PICKING UP SUPPLIES

I used the Animated Signal Corp. FC100 flasher circuit, but any flasher that works with light-emitting diodes (LEDs) and runs on 6 to 9 volts DC is okay. Also get some fine wire that will slide through the brass tubes in the crossing signal kit. The rest of the supplies needed are shown in the "Products used" table.

BUILDING THE SIGNALS

I built the signals pretty much as the kit instructions suggested. Instead of the black plastic crossbucks that came with the kit, I used preprinted white crossbucks from Oregon Rail Supply's kit no. 112, just to save some work. I also changed the way the LEDs are attached.

Before doing any soldering on the LEDs, I checked their fit in the targets. Mine were a bit snug, so I trimmed around the inside of the targets with a knife until the LEDs slid in smoothly.

When soldering electronics keep three things in mind: use rosin-core solder, get in and out quickly, and apply enough heat so you don't get a "cold" joint. I like to use small-diameter rosin-core solder. A 25-watt soldering iron will provide more than enough heat for the thin solder to make a good joint.

LIGHT-EMITTING DIODES

Every LED has two leads called electrodes. The negative electrode is called the cathode; the positive one is called the anode. Cathodes are identified by being longer, having a tab, or by a flat spot on the round base of the LED. On the LEDs that came with my Oregon signal kit, the longer lead marks the cathode.

Because of the flasher circuit I used, I didn't solder the anodes of the LEDs together as suggested in the Oregon kit. Rather, I soldered the opposite leads together. Figure 1 shows how the LEDs are located and connected to the mast.

After everything except the crossbucks was fastened to the mast, I soldered another 12" length of wire to the bottom of the mast.

If you're like me and don't trust your wiring, you can skip down to the wiring section and bench-test your signals before installation. Test both signals at the same time, or they'll appear to flash too fast.

I brush-painted my signals with Floquil Old Silver. To paint the targets and banner board — the "STOP ON RED SIGNAL" sign — I used a Tamiya Flat Black paint pen. It's water-based so if you get paint where it's not wanted, just wet your finger and rub the paint off before it dries.

Next I added the printed crossbucks to the assembly, and applied the decals to the banner board. After the decals had dried, I sprayed the signals with Testor's Dullcote to seal the lettering.

PREPARING THE SITE

To help me position the signals so a passing train wouldn't hit them, I used

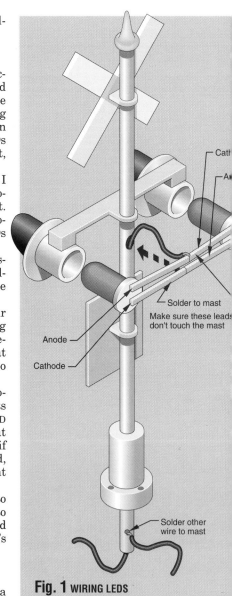

Cathode

Anode

Solder to mast
Make sure these leads don't touch the mast

Anode

Cathode

Solder other wire to mast

Fig. 1 WIRING LEDS

a National Model Railroad Association (NMRA) HO scale standards gauge. You can find the standards gauge at most hobby shops.

Next I drilled a ⅛" hole for each signal, carefully pushed the signal wires through with a small screwdriver, and inserted the base of the signal mast to be sure it fit. Then I lifted the signal until it was barely out of its hole, applied Goo to the bottom of the mast, and slid the signal back into place, making sure the wires went through first.

The Radio Shack push button needs a ½" hole on the edge of the layout. Drill the hole low enough so there are no obstructions behind the switch. Before I installed the button, I soldered two 12" wires to it. I secured the button with Goo.

WIRING

Figure 2 shows the basic layout of the components and how they're connected.

The only wire-to-wire connections should be the leads from the switch to the battery. A right-angle "pigtail" twist should hold these together for soldering.

I insulated my wire-to-wire solder connection with heat-shrink tubing. Heat-shrink tubing does what its name implies — it shrinks when heated. I picked a size from the Radio Shack assortment that would barely slide over the solder connection. A 1,250-watt hair dryer with a concentrator provides enough heat to shrink the tubing.

The FC100 flasher circuit has input lugs for 6 and 12 volts. I used the 6-volt lug with the 9-volt battery. You're probably saying, "Won't that burn up the circuit?" Yes and no. The FC100 can regulate the higher voltage for a short time before overheating. Using the 9-volt battery in short bursts instead of continuously keeps the circuit from failing. If the circuit does get too hot and malfunctions, let it sit for a while. It will probably work again after everything has cooled down.

To keep hot solder from falling in my face, I did most of my soldering before I fastened the components to the layout. I attached all components under the layout with double-sided foam tape strips.

With the wiring connected, I installed a fresh battery and tested my circuit. If your flashers don't work when you press the push-button switch, check for the following:

• Good battery connections?
• Polarity correct?
• LED leads not touching?
• All connections made properly?

If you still can't find the problem, disconnect one flasher at a time and see if the other works. If it does, check for shorting on the disconnected flasher. If it doesn't, recheck the circuit with the other flasher.

FINISHING TOUCHES

When the flashers work correctly we can add the little details that complete the scene. Most real grade crossings have at least a white line painted on the pavement for motorists to stay behind. Some crossings even have "RXR" painted on the street, which is what I decided to do. I used a white map pencil and a straightedge to draw the lines on the road.

Then I installed a Trackside Parts small relay box next to the signal at the edge of the layout. There's usually only one of these boxes per crossing on the prototype, and it contains all the "smarts" and batteries for the crossing signals. Yeah, the real ones work on batteries too!

After you've finished testing the signals, stand back and enjoy how the grade crossing looks when you push the button. Next month Art Curren will show you how to fill a corner with different stores. ⌀

Products used

Animated Signal Corp.
FC100 flasher circuit

Floquil paint
110100 Old Silver

Oregon Rail Supply
112 crossbucks
113 crossing flashers

Radio Shack
64-005 .032" rosin-core solder
64-2344 double-sided tape strips
270-325 9-volt battery clips
270-326 9-volt battery holder
275-1566 momentary push-button soft-feel switch
278-1627 heat-shrink tubing

Tamiya
XF-1 Flat Black paint pen

Testor Corp.
1260 Dullcote spray

Trackside Parts
180 small relay box

Wm. K. Walthers
299 Goo

Miscellaneous
28-gauge wire

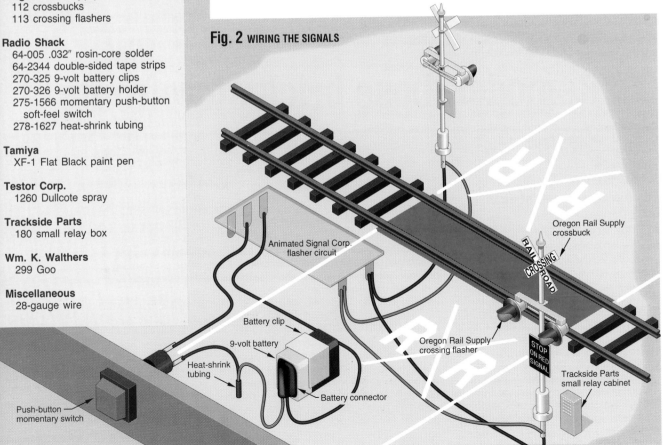

Fig. 2 WIRING THE SIGNALS

Animated Signal Corp. flasher circuit

Battery clip

9-volt battery

Heat-shrink tubing

Battery connector

Push-button momentary switch

Oregon Rail Supply crossbuck

Oregon Rail Supply crossing flasher

STOP ON RED SIGNAL

Trackside Parts small relay cabinet

Adding a small block of stores proved to be a simple yet effective way of filling up a vacant corner on our HO scale Cripple Creek Central project layout.

Remodel those brick storefronts

Modified, detailed kit buildings for a corner of our HO project layout

BY ART CURREN
PHOTOS BY A. L. SCHMIDT

THIS MONTH we're going to do a little "upgrading" in two ways: First, we'll upgrade a couple of storefronts by giving them a face-lift; second, we'll place the buildings on a street with a grade. The new storefronts let us retain the charm of the older-style architecture and at the same time bring the buildings into more modern times. This is something often found in older towns as stores are renovated.

The finished scene fits neatly into the city corner of our HO scale Cripple Creek Central project layout between the track and the edge of the table. This technique will work on other layouts as well.

STRUCTURES

We begin with two Design Preservation Models Kelly's Saloon kits and one Goodfellows Hall kit. To get your feet wet, assemble one saloon kit according to the instructions and set it aside.

We'll modernize the second saloon kit by adding an aluminum front (actually Evergreen V-groove siding) to replace the older storefront. Start by sawing off the old storefront just above the fancy trim below the three windows, using the trim as a guide for a razor saw. Once you've done this, assemble the building and cut a piece of V-groove siding to fit the gap in the front. Measure in three grooves from each side and 1/2" from the top, then cut out this opening. File the cut edges smooth. Build the front as shown in fig. 1.

I used two AM Models doors placed side by side. I opened up the left door by cutting and filing out the center. I finished the door as in fig. 1. The width of the doors determines the width of the new store window.

After assembling the front, I masked off the floor, back, and side of the showroom window box with tape and sprayed the whole front with Testor's Aluminum. After the paint had dried, I added the window glass. I filed my window to a force-fit in the opening, but a little styrene cement can be flowed along the seams from the inside. Add clear styrene to the back of the open door and set the completed front aside.

TILE-FRONT BUILDING

The Goodfellows Hall kit was too deep to fit in our tight space, so I removed a

½″ section from each side wall before assembling the building. Next I sawed off the older front on the right side where the new tile front would go. Figure 1 shows how I used Evergreen tile to make the new front.

I scratchbuilt the door using various sizes of strip styrene, but a Pikestuff no. 1106 door (or other commercial door) could be substituted easily. Adjust the tile opening to fit the door you use. Don't cut the tile squares in half — if your door is smaller than the opening, add styrene shims to fill the space.

I painted the door and shims Aluminum, and "painted" the tiles with a green felt-tip marker. Any green that gets into the grooves is easily removed with a sharp hobby knife. File the front to a snug force-fit in the opening and set it aside.

PAINTING AND WEATHERING

Before adding the new fronts I painted and weathered the structures. The brick surfaces on the two outside buildings were painted with Floquil SP *Daylight* Red, and the middle one with Rust. I used Light Green for the trim on the repair store and Roof Brown on the flower shop. The large building comes molded in a light tan, so I left the trim that color and painted only the window sills (Concrete) and lintels (Oxide Red). I used Concrete for the sills and lintels on the smaller buildings. All roofs are Grimy Black.

To weather the flower shop and Goodfellows buildings, I applied a wash of India ink in alcohol. Then I sprayed all three structures with Testor's Dullcote and added a wash of Polly S White. Washes are pigment (ink or paint) thinned with lots of water or alcohol. I use a mix of about 10 to 15 parts thinner to 1 part paint. You can always add one wash on top of another, so a light wash is better than one that's too dark. The clear "glass" and new fronts can now be added to the buildings. Secure these with liquid plastic cement.

A STREET ON A HILL

Once the buildings were assembled I placed them side by side on our small triangular corner to determine where the street could go. For the scenic base we used 1″-thick Styrofoam insulation as shown in fig. 2. The dimensions of your base will depend on the space you have. Keep the edge of the base about an inch from the edge of the roadbed. Locate the structure foundations and glue them in place.

I used a hacksaw blade — just the blade, not the saw — to cut a slope in the upper Styrofoam layer to blend it with the lower layer. Cut on the pulling stroke with the teeth pointing toward you. This formed the roadway.

Next, I added another foundation of

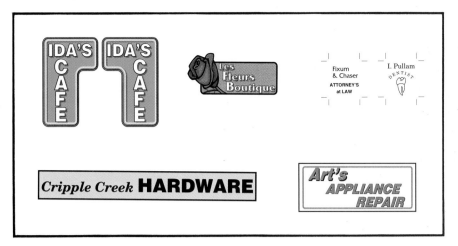

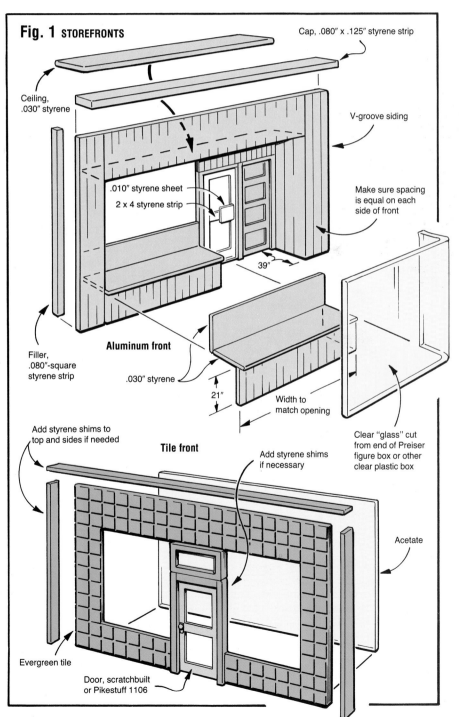

Fig. 1 STOREFRONTS

Cap, .080″ x .125″ styrene strip

Ceiling, .030″ styrene

V-groove siding

.010″ styrene sheet

2 x 4 styrene strip

Make sure spacing is equal on each side of front

39″

Filler, .080″-square styrene strip

Aluminum front

.030″ styrene

21″

Width to match opening

Clear "glass" cut from end of Preiser figure box or other clear plastic box

Add styrene shims to top and sides if needed

Tile front

Add styrene shims if necessary

Acetate

Evergreen tile

Door, scratchbuilt or Pikestuff 1106

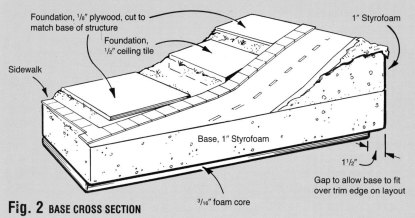

Styrofoam base goes to the layout's edge. Paint the base's exposed edges with tan latex.

Foundation, 1/8" plywood, cut to match base of structure

Foundation, 1/2" ceiling tile

Sidewalk

1" Styrofoam

Base, 1" Styrofoam

Gap to allow base to fit over trim edge on layout

1 1/2"

3/16" foam core

Fig. 2 BASE CROSS SECTION

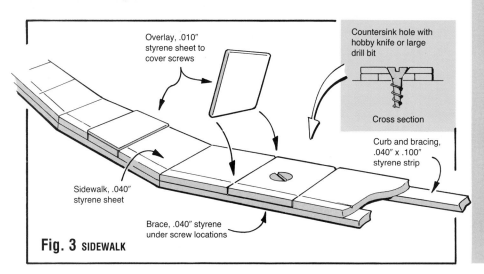

Overlay, .010" styrene sheet to cover screws

Countersink hole with hobby knife or large drill bit

Cross section

Curb and bracing, .040" x .100" styrene strip

Sidewalk, .040" styrene sheet

Brace, .040" styrene under screw locations

Fig. 3 SIDEWALK

.100" x .250" styrene strip to each structure, then placed the buildings in position. To make the sidewalk I made a template of heavy paper to match the sidewalk edge to the curve and the fronts of the buildings. I transferred this outline to a sheet of .040" styrene.

Draw a parallel line 6 feet from the line marking the building edge of the sidewalk. Using a hobby knife, scribe both lines on the styrene and cut out the sidewalk by bending and snapping the styrene at these lines.

File the edges of the styrene square and use a knife to scribe in the sidewalk squares. Scribe the curb line first and the sidewalk segments next to meet the curb line. I added a few random cracks. Figure 3 shows the rest of the sidewalk construction. Once the sidewalk is done, place it in front of the buildings and check its fit. I used three screws to fasten it at the top, middle, and bottom.

As the photos show, I added other sidewalks for access to the rear doorways. These were done in a similar fashion.

Where these walks meet the main sidewalk, I added steps from .100" x .125" styrene. I also added some small steps in front of doorways on the large building.

Raising the foundations required adding small styrene floors to the foundations under the doorways in the two upper buildings. Paint all the foundations and sidewalks a concrete color. I used a mix of Floquil Antique White with a few drops of Roof Brown and Concrete added. An India-ink wash darkens everything into a nice concrete color.

SCENERY AND STREET

Make the street from premixed spackling compound. Spread it on with a putty knife and let it harden. Sand the rough spots, then use a wet paper towel to smooth the surface. The wet towel will soften the spackle and smooth the surface even after it has set. Paint the road with a gray latex paint.

The rear edge of the hill runs down close to the tracks. Cut it to shape with the hacksaw blade. As fig. 4 shows, I added a couple of retaining walls behind the buildings, and the highest building required another extension of the foundation and a set of steps. All were made from styrene and painted with the concrete mix.

The center building has a retaining wall made from Kibri's stone-textured plastic sheet. I cut this to fit and fastened it to the structure's foundation. Then I added another sidewalk behind these buildings with porches and steps made from various sizes of styrene.

For the iron railings I used a handrail set from an Athearn diesel. The white wooden railings use .060" x .060" posts and 2 x 4 horizontal members. Figure 5 shows how to make the lower retaining walls and loading platform.

Apply dirt, grass, and ground foam weeds as we've done in previous installments. The scenicking can be done with the buildings out of the way. If gaps appear between the building foundations and scenery, fill them with thin cardboard and reapply scenery. Small pieces of ground foam and weeds will hide gaps.

FINAL DETAILS

I painted the window shades from behind (various colors will do). Other details include chimney flues and soil pipes (round sprues with holes drilled into the ends) and roof hatches (styrene rectangles). The picket fence with gate is from the building we kitbashed in the June 1991 MODEL RAILROADER.

After mounting the signs on .030" styrene, I glued them to the buildings. The small signs in the windows are glued on the inside. The protruding da's Cafe sign is mounted on .080" styrene, with holes drilled in the rear edge and pins inserted. I then drilled corresponding holes into the building to receive the pins and secure the sign.

Since these buildings are at the front edge of the layout, some interior detail seemed necessary. The easiest was the curtain in the cafe. It's a piece of clear styrene with the "curtains" drybrushed vertically using white typewriter correction fluid. Then I brushed it again with a yellow felt-tip pen. The piece was mounted across the window opening with a .060" x .060" strip at the base to keep it a short distance behind the window glass.

Fig. 4. RETAINING WALLS. The concrete retaining walls were made from sheet styrene. Use an assortment of colors and textures of ground foam to blend the base with the layout table.

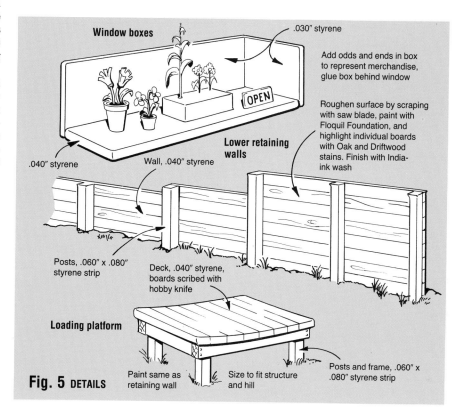

Fig. 5 DETAILS

In the florist's window I placed some ground foam, a few pots made from sprues, and material from a plastic aquarium plant. I painted on flowers with dabs of white correction fluid and red nail polish. The other windows needed boxes added behind them as shown in fig. 5. All kinds of junk (mostly sprues) can be added in the boxes to represent the wares of the store. A shovel and a wheelbarrow are about the only "real" things in the hardware store's window.

Add pieces of black construction paper across the full inside width of the buildings to act as view blocks.

Installing the hill was easy. I placed it in position and secured it with screws from under the layout board. Coarse ground foam will hide the joint between the hill and layout board. Once the hill is in place, add a few cracks in the street with a fine-point felt-tip pen. Place some figures and vehicles in the scene, and you'll have an upgraded block of stores. ☒

How to operate a small layout realistically

Scenario cards for a different train every time

BY JIM KELLY
PHOTOS BY CHRIS BECKER

In this last chapter of our Cripple Creek Central series, we start running the HO layout like a real railroad. Scenario cards tell us the number and type of cars needed in a train.

L ET'S START with a definition: Operation is running trains on a model railroad in a purposeful manner, the same as they would be run on a real railroad. You imagine that your railroad connects with the rest of the world and trains come and go delivering cars to destinations on or beyond your layout.

Operation is a game that can be simpler than checkers or more complex than three-dimensional chess, but with one very important difference — you make it all up yourself. You make the game board (your layout) and the game pieces (cars and locomotives) and establish the rules. If you want to get deep into the subject, read Bruce Chubb's book *How to Operate your Model Railroad* (Kalmbach Publishing Co.).

Operation on a basement-sized layout can be quite complex, with sessions that last for hours and involve a dozen or more operators. Obviously this level of activity isn't possible on a small layout like our HO scale Cripple Creek Central, but if you give it a try, you'll be surprised just how engrossing running the daily local can be. It can easily involve two operators, one playing the engineer, another the brakeman.

THE LAYOUT AS A RAILROAD

To get started let's stop looking at the layout as a circle of track and start thinking of it more as a real railroad. If we straighten the loop in our imaginations, we have the railroad shown in fig. 1.

Allen Jct. is our interchange with the Denver & Rio Grande Western, whose

S-2 locomotive we've been leasing since our old GP9 broke a crankshaft.

All the cars that run on our railroad come on and go off at Allen Jct. This we accomplish by hand, using what modelers since ancient times have been calling "the old 0-5-0." The cars we take off can be stored in boxes or on shelves under the layout.

MAKING UP A TRAIN

Okay, so how do we make up a train? For an answer let's turn to real railroading, or as we often call it, the prototype. Real railroads deliver cars because they've been asked to. This can be on a very informal basis. For example, the manager at a small packing plant calls to say he has a boxcar loaded with hides and ready to go to the tannery. Or the arrangement can be much larger and more formal. Perhaps the railroad has negotiated a contract with an assembly

plant to transport thousands of auto rack cars loaded with new automobiles over the course of several years.

To develop a scheme let's make a list of the industries our railroad serves as well as the types of loads they normally receive and originate. See fig. 2. Note that the team track (a name that goes back to horses and wagons) serves imaginary off-line industries. You can make up as many of these as you'd like and serve them with virtually any sort of cars. Goods delivered to this track are transferred to trucks and continue to their destinations.

After we've listed our industries, we can make another list of possible daily scenarios, as shown in fig. 3. Most days will be routine. Tews Cement, for example, receives two loads of cement and two loads of gravel on a typical day. There'll be other days, though, that are exceptions, and we've listed some of these as

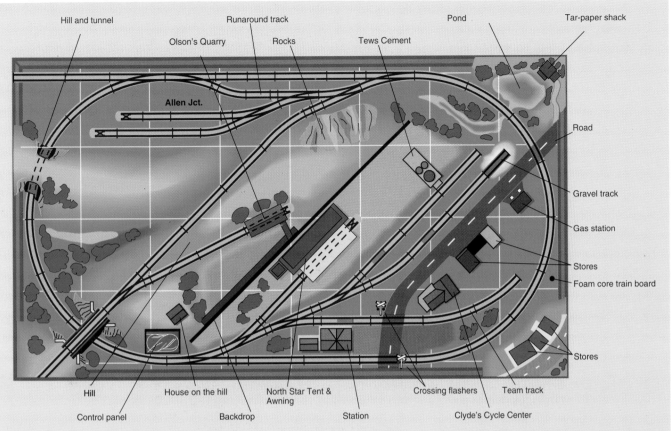

Hill and tunnel · Runaround track · Pond · Tar-paper shack
Olson's Quarry · Rocks · Tews Cement
Allen Jct.
Road
Gravel track
Gas station
Stores
Foam core train board
Stores
Hill · House on the hill · North Star Tent & Awning · Crossing flashers · Team track
Control panel · Backdrop · Station · Clyde's Cycle Center

Cripple Creek Central RR

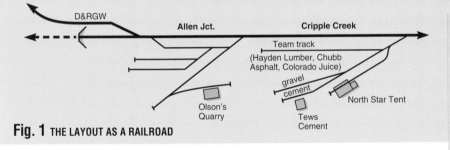

D&RGW
Allen Jct.
Cripple Creek
Team track
(Hayden Lumber, Chubb
Asphalt, Colorado Juice)
gravel
cement
North Star Tent
Olson's
Quarry
Tews
Cement

Fig. 1 THE LAYOUT AS A RAILROAD

Fig. 2 CRIPPLE CREEK INDUSTRIES

Industry	Receives	Ships
Olson's Quarry	empty hoppers, machinery	crushed stone, gravel, Olsonite
Tews Cement	cement, gravel, sand	0
North Star Tent	canvas, plastic pellets, vinyl	tents, flags, awnings
Team Track		
Colorado Juice	frozen concentrate	0
Hayden Building Supply	lumber	0
Chubb Driveways	asphalt	0

well. Note that on some days a few industries get no cars at all.

Next we'll fill in some 3 x 5 index cards, like those shown in fig. 4. Note that we make four or five cards for a typical scenario, only one for a rarer one. Think of each card as representing a phone conversation with a plant manager. We mix up the cards for each industry, then put them in a file box.

To make up a train we first pull the front card for an industry, place the car or cars required on the track, and write them down on our switch list. The card pulled goes to the back of the pack for that particular industry.

THE BIG CAR SHORTAGE

In putting this Scenario Card System to the test, I quickly came to a surprising and pleasant realization. I didn't have nearly enough cars and had to borrow a bunch from our MODEL RAILROADER

club layout. The trains I was making up averaged six to eight cars, and that many more would already be on the layout, placed there by the previous train.

We'd like not to see the same cars appearing at the same places over and over, so a roster of several dozen cars or more would be desirable. Most of us like to buy and build cars anyway, so that's great. Meanwhile we'll operate with what we have. If a card calls for a car we don't have, we'll just carry on without it.

Let's say you need a boxcar for the tent company. Which one do you choose? You could make cards for the cars and draw them at random, but probably the easiest way is to use the one that's been off the layout the longest.

LET'S RUN A TRAIN

Our crew reports to work at the station in Cripple Creek. We talk to the agent and pick up the switch list. Then,

after a quick cup of coffee, we walk over to the engine and caboose, usually kept on the gravel track at Tews. We pull out of Cripple Creek, then back around to the interchange.

Arriving at Allen Jct. we check the switch list against the cars left off during the night by the Rio Grande (fig. 5). Any cars destined for the quarry we leave behind. The rest are pulled back to Cripple Creek (fig. 6).

Once there we put our caboose in some convenient hole and start switching. One good way is to work from industry to industry, first pulling the empties, then switching in the loads. When we've finished we leave town and back the empties around to and

Industry	Scenario and number of cards		Industry	Scenario and number of cards	
North Star Tent	Receive 1 boxcar canvas, 1 hopper plastic pellets	5	Olson's Quarry	Receive 2 gravel cars	8
	Receive 1 boxcar canvas	2		Receive 3 gravel cars	3
	Receive 2 boxcars canvas	3		Receive 2 gravel cars, 1 flatcar (machinery)	1
	0 (nothing today)	3		Receive 1 gravel car	1
	Receive 1 boxcar canvas, 1 flatcar (machinery)	1		Receive 1 gravel car, 1 boxcar (Olsonite loading)	1
Chubb Driveways	Receive 1 tank car asphalt	2	Tews Cement	Receive 2 cement cars, 1 gravel car	8
	0 (nothing today)	4		Receive 2 cement cars, 2 gravel cars	3
Colorado Juice	Receive 1 plug-door box, concentrate	3		Receive 2 cement cars, 1 boxcar (additives)	1
	0 (nothing today)	3		Receive 1 cement car, 1 gravel car	1
Hayden Building	Receive 1 boxcar lumber	4		Receive 3 cement cars	1
	Receive 1 bulkhead flat	3		Receive 3 cement cars, 1 gravel car	1
	0 (nothing today)	5			

Fig. 3 DAILY SCENARIOS

past the interchange. (We have a rule against going through the tunnel to get from Cripple Creek to the junction or vice versa, as doing so would spoil our point-to-point illusion. Once at the junction, though, we're allowed to back into the tunnel, as we're not doing so to reach Cripple Creek.)

RUNAROUND MOVES

So far our moves have been easy because they all involved backing in and out of spurs on what railroaders call trailing switches. Getting cars into the quarry, though, calls for a facing switch move, and to make it we must first run around the cars to get the locomotive behind them. See fig. 7. To complicate matters, our tail track at the quarry is short and we must take the cars up and down two at a time.

First we run up and bring down the loaded cars. Then we run around them and tack them onto the train we're leaving for the Rio Grande. We pull the empty gravel cars from the siding and spot them on the runaround track. Then we run around those cars and take them up the hill.

Our stomachs are beginning to growl as we gather up our caboose and spot the train so the Rio Grande's 0-5-0 can take it away. Then we head back for Cripple Creek and a late lunch at Ida's Cafe followed by a few games of eight ball over at the pool hall.

Fig. 4. SCENARIO CARDS. Following the guidelines that we established in fig. 3, we filled out 3 x 5 cards for each industry and placed them in this file box. As we draw a card for each industry, we select the cars that we'll use and write them down on our switch list. Readers are welcome to make copies.

Fig. 5. STARTING OUT. Our engine crew arrives at Allen Jct. on a typical workday. These cars have been dropped off by the Rio Grande for delivery to sites on our railroad.

Switch list   Date: _____

Car no.	Type	Destination	√

Fig. 6. ENTERING TOWN. The seven cars already sitting on spurs in Cripple Creek will be going back to Allen Jct. after we've finished switching the industries.

A FLEXIBLE SYSTEM

Try this Scenario Card System, and I think you'll like it. It's extremely flexible. As you add or subtract industries, just throw out the affected old cards and make new ones. If your trains are too long for your taste, take out cards that call for multiple cars and add more "0" (nothing today) cards. In short order you'll find the system giving you the kinds of trains you like to run, yet each train and each operating session will be different.

This article concludes our series on the Cripple Creek Central. There's lots more that could be done, but we'll leave those things up to you. We hope you've enjoyed watching the layout grow. If this series helped you get started on your first layout or provided some project you enjoyed, we're delighted. And rest assured there'll be lots of information for beginners in future issues of MR. ◘

Our engine has brought two loaded gravel cars down from Olson's Quarry and spotted them on the runaround track. Now it's time to run around them and add them to the string of cars extending through the tunnel.

Fig. 7 TYPICAL RUNAROUND MOVE

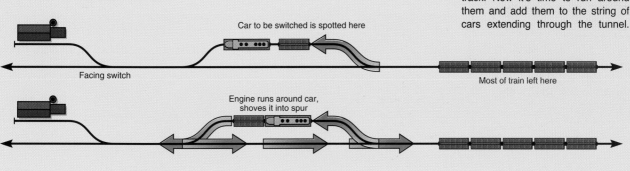

Car to be switched is spotted here

Facing switch

Most of train left here

Engine runs around car, shoves it into spur

Addresses

Alexander Scale Models
P.O. Box 7121
Grand Rapids, MI 49507

Alloy Forms
P.O. Box 1421
Golden, CO 80402

Amaco (American Art Clay Co.)
4717 W. 16th Street
Indianapolis, IN 46222

Animated Signal Corp.
P.O. Box 1342
Maple Grove, MN 55311

Athearn Inc.
19010 Laurel Park Road
Compton, CA 90222

Atlas Model Railroad Inc.
378 Florence Ave.
Hillside, NJ 07205

Bachman Industries Inc.
1400 E. Erie Ave.
Philadelphia, PA 19124

Con-Cor International
P.O. Box 328
Bensonville, IL 60106

Design Preservation Models
P.O. Box 280
Crestone, CO 81131

AM Models (available through Walters) Eastern Car Works
P.O. Box "L" 624
Langhorne, PA 19047

Faller (available through Walthers)

Floquil-Polly S Color Corp.
Route 30 N.
Amsterdam, NY 12010

Funaro & Camerlengo
R.D. 3, Box 2800
Honesdale, PA 18431

Grandt Line Products
1040-B Shary Court
Concord, CA 94518

Kadee Quality Products
P.O. Box 1726
Medford, OR 97501

Kato U.S.A. Inc.
781 Dillon Drive
Wood Dale, IL 60191

Kibri (available through Walthers)

Life-Like Products Inc.
1600 Union Ave.
Baltimore, MD 21211

Highball Products
P.O. Box 43633
Cincinnati, OH 45243

Mantua Metal Products Co.
Grandview Ave.
Woodbury Heights, NJ 08097

Model Rectifier Corp.
200 Carter Drive, P.O. Box 267
Edison, NJ 08818

Model Die Casting Inc.
P.O. Box 926
Hawthorne, CA 90251

Mascot Precision Tools
750 Washington Ave.
Carlstadt, NJ 07072

Model Power
180 Smith Street
Farmingdale, NY 11735

Magnuson Models (available through Walthers)

Northeastern Scale Models
99 Cross Street, P.O. Box 425
Methuen, MA 01844

NJ International
77 W Nicholai Street
Hicksville, NY 11801

Oregon Rail Supply
7212 N. Olympia
Portland, OR 97203

Pacer Technology & Resources
9420 Santa Anita Ave.
Rancho Cucamonga, CA 91730

Pactra Hobby
1000 Lake Road
Medina, OH 44256

Pikestuff
7700 Huckleberry Lane
Evansville, IN 47712

Polyterrain
HC66, Box 93
Wittier, AR 72776

Paul M. Preiser KG
Postfach 1233, D-8803
Rothenburg o.d.T., West Germany

Scalecoat, div. of Quality Craft Models Inc.
177 Wheatley Ave.
Northumberland, PA 17857

Testor Corp.
620 Buckbee Street
Rockford, IL 61104

Trackside Parts
55 Alvin Street
Providence, RI 02907

Wm. K. Walthers Inc.
P.O. Box 18676
Milwaukee, WI 53218

Westerfield
Route 2, Box 374
River Road, Crossville, TN 38555

Woodland Scenics
P.O. Box 98
Linn Creek, MO 65052

X-acto Inc., div of Hunt Mfg. Co.
230 S. Broad Street
Philadelphia, PA 19102

Index